The Investment Game in Private Equity

International Banking and Securities Law

Volume published in this Brill Research Perspectives title are listed at *brill.com/rpbs*

The Investment Game in Private Equity

By

Mika J. Lehtimäki

TUTA SUB AEGIDE PALLAS · 1683 ·

BRILL

LEIDEN | BOSTON

This paperback book edition is simultaneously published as issue 4.1 of *International Banking and Securities Law* DOI: 10.1163/24056936-12340010.

Library of Congress Control Number: 2022933812

Brill Open Access options can be found at brill.com/openaccess.

Typeface for the Latin, Greek, and Cyrillic scripts: "Brill". See and download: brill.com/brill-typeface.

ISBN 978-90-04-51463-8 (paperback)
ISBN 978-90-04-51784-4 (e-book)

This book is printed on acid-free paper and produced in a sustainable manner.

Contents

The Investment Game in Private Equity

Mika J. Lehtimäki
DPhil, Oxford; Partner, Attorneys-at-Law TRUST
Mika.Lehtimaki@icloud.com

Abstract

Private equity investing and the relationship between the GP and the LPs are plagued with the risk of information asymmetries and agency costs, so the markets have developed several mechanisms to align the incentives of the funds and the investors, most importantly through disclosure and protections in limited partnership agreements. However, such agreements may not always deal with the most important asymmetries or agency conflicts, especially the hidden effort problem. From the fund's perspective, there are also other relationships that affect its internal dynamics. They are the need for interest alignment between the fund (and the GP) and the managers of the portfolio companies, the risk of financial agency costs and the risk of strategic creditor actions. All of these relationships are regulated primarily by contracts. In this paper, I evaluate the game-theoretical framework, Investment Game, based on the analysis of the GP-LP investment-effort relationship supported by a brief analysis of the other relationships. I argue that, in most cases, the LPs are able to solve the GP effort maximisation problem making part of the fund regulation unnecessary. However, private ordering may not work in some cases. Despite these situations, the Investment Game enables, even when the LPs cannot affect the fund terms, an analysis of the GP effort level and the level of undisclosed private benefits. Therefore, the Investment Game also sets a framework for a data analysis of private equity investing.

Keywords

private equity – game theory – AIFM – fund regulation – financial law – regulatory analysis

 | DOI:10.1163/9789004517844_002

1 Introduction

1.1 *An Example of Misalignment of Interests*

Let's assume that a pension insurance company has invested 100 million euros in a private equity fund of 1 billion euros. The fund has made a total of ten investments during its investment period. Two of the acquisitions by the fund become distressed. The investment manager learns that the firm affiliated with the general partner has charged a total of 90 million as transaction fees from the fund. Also, a distressed fund managed by the same fund group has provided rescue financing for the group together with its original senior lenders, which now hold a majority of the surviving entity's shares. Despite these events, fund produces a total return of 17% per annum, exceeding the hurdle rate of 8%. There is a catch-up in the limited partnership agreement ensuring distribution of post-capital return income 80% to the limited partners and 20% to the general partner.[1]

Should the pension insurance company be happy with the return of the fund or be concerned about the fees, the restructuring outcomes and the director compensation? The chief investment officer asks, why don't these issues come up by fund monitoring, and why the risk-adjusted return of the LPs is so different from that of the fund manager?

From the fund's perspective, the answers appear straight-forward. First, the return levels of the GP and the LPs are contractual, and any return received by the LP above the hurdle rate represents alpha created by the fund.[2] The management fees, on the other hand, are required to run the day-to-day operations of the fund and, because holding periods are long, the GP will have to ensure adequate management resources for the period. In relation to the compensation, the value-creation of the fund is founded on the alignment of the interests of the managers with the fund. As for the transaction fees, corporate M&A is cost-heavy with lawyer accountant and process-related fees, which are material for ensuring exceptional transaction advise. Furthermore, LBO restructurings are complex transactions, in which the parties try their best to

1 See for an example Institutional Limited Partners Association ILPA, *ILPA Principles 3.0: Fostering Transparency, Governance and Alignment of Interests for General and Limited Partners* (2019) 100.

2 A contractually fixed hurdle rate does not naturally represent the actual market return with the similar risk profile but a rough estimation of that. The levels and the incentives caused by fixed hurdle rates in limited partnerships have been subject to much debate over the last years, arguably it is a material question. See e.g.: Ludovic Phalippou, 'Modifying The Carried Interest To Do What It Is Said To Do (February 12, 2019)' Available at SSRN: https://ssrncom/abstract=3333053.

maintain value for the fund. Would the above actions not be in the interests of the LPs? Therefore, the effort and compensation of the GP should be well-aligned with the LPs.

The above exemplifies some of the recurring themes arising between the fund and its stakeholders. However, the objectives of asset management and fund management regulation often extend far beyond these concerns e.g. to informing the portfolio company employees,[3] rules on restrictions on selling the assets of the portfolio companies,[4] using depositaries, and remuneration. Also, when the number of funds and their assets under management grow, failure of a fund or their over-leveraging may have systemic effects.[5] This may justify broader intervention into the operations of the fund manager, the fund itself and its investments.[6] When we discuss the scope of fund regulation, we should note that the main target of regulatory emphasis varies somewhat from jurisdiction to jurisdiction. For example in the EU, the most important piece of regulation applying to private equity fund management, i.e. the Alternative Fund Managers Directive ("AIFMD"), regulates primarily the fund managers themselves (later "AIFM") and not, with some exceptions, the actual funds. There is very little product-specific or fund unit-specific regulation in the AIFMD.

Despite the jurisdiction specific emphasis on different aspects on fund management, there are certain core features that asset management and fund legislation will necessarily have to address.[7] Such core features concern the impact of fund operation on the investors and the society as a whole and addressing these through conduct of business, transparency, disclosure, and systemic risks rules.[8] Except for the systemic risk, which has a broad scope, the

3 See e.g. Directive 2011/61/EU of the European Parliament and of the Council of 8 June 2011 on Alternative Investment Fund Managers and amending Directives 2003/41/EC and 2009/65/EC and Regulations (EC) No 1060/2009 and (EU) No 1095/2010 (the "AIFMD") article 27(4).

4 E.g. AIFMD, article 30.

5 See AIFMD e.g. articles 15(1), 24, 25 and 53.

6 From the legal perspective the relevant issues concern primarily fund structuring and tax, prudential and capital/liquidity regulation, liability questions, fund offering rules, rules concerning share issues and incentive schemes as well as financial and insolvency law issues. Because most of these legal questions are specific to the particular relationships among the fund and its stakeholders, it is logical to analyse them separately, subject to relationship-specific regulatory and legal objectives.

7 For example, it is stated in Preamble 2 of the AIFMD that it "aims at establishing common requirements governing the authorisation and supervision of AIFMs in order to provide a coherent approach to the related risks and their impact on investors and markets in the Union."

8 Jennifer Payne, 'Private Equity and Its Regulation in Europe' 12 EUROPEAN BUSINESS ORGANIZATION LAW REVIEW, 570–71. See of the rationale of different type of regulation in Singapore: Lin Lin, 'Private Equity in Singapore' SSRN Electronic Journal, 5–8.

core functions are connected to at least three theoretical questions: adverse selection (hidden information) problem, the moral hazard (hidden action) problem and the agency costs arising in fund management.[9] Understanding these problems is material for any fund regulatory analysis.

1.2 *The Objective and Structure of the Paper*

1.2.1 Scope of the Analysis

In this paper, I examine one core objective of fund regulation, i.e. controlling risks that private equity funds impose on their investors. More specifically, I analyse under what conditions and whether the incentive structures of the funds deviate from those of the investors. If these incentives can be aligned in a free contracting environment, it can be argued that the scope of prudential regulation as well as e.g. conduct of business and remuneration rules should be limited.[10]

The analysis is carried out from the perspective of the 'investment game' between the general partner (GP)[11] of the fund and the limited partners (LP) of the fund (the Investment Game). The central feature of the Investment Game is evaluating whether the LPs can control the asymmetric information and agency costs problems contractually. The GP-LP analysis is supported by discussion of the incentives and decision-making procedures, on the one hand, between the GP and the managers of the portfolio companies the fund holds and, on the other hand, between the GP, and the creditors of the portfolio companies.

The objective of this analysis is to evaluate whether there exist specific Nash equilibria,[12] or another type of a game-theoretical equilibria, in the parties' strategies under the Investment Game that results from the market practice and contracts. The Investment Game is an extensive form of a game with the objective of maximising the parties' investment outcomes. The nature and conditions of the Nash equilibria in the Investment Game enable us to analyse whether they lead to a Pareto optimal result and what role fund regulation can

9 See Section 3.

10 I will not discuss in this paper the questions of systemic risk relating to asset management, although the findings presented may have effects on this question as well.

11 Because the management is often divided between the GP, the advisory firm and other affiliated entities, I will refer to all of these collectively as the GP.

12 Nash equilibrium is finding the best strategy taking into consideration the best strategies of other players. See generally on the definition in the relevant legal context: D. G. Baird, RH Gertner and RC Picker, *Game Theory and the Law* (Harvard University Press 1994) 21–23.

play, if any, in Pareto improving[13] these outcomes.[14] The focus of the AIFMD on the regulation of management entities, instead of the funds themselves, fits well with the Investment Game analysis because the actions and decisions taken by the relevant parties in the game are those made by the management entity or an advisory company to which the investment management functions are outsourced.[15]

I will focus in this paper on funds investing into equity of acquired portfolio companies where the acquisition is heavily leveraged. One of the main forms of such acquisitions is a leveraged-buy-out (LBO).

1.2.2 The Main Argument

I argue that LPs can solve the GP effort maximisation problem by private ordering making a part of the fund management regulation unnecessary or inefficient. If the maximisation problem is solved, but this leads to non-investment, it is not a failure of a contractual regime but a common failure to reach a commercial deal. The analysis will show that the GPs are economically incentivised to disclose their effort level, pre-commit to that and to provide the LPs optimal amount of information and transparency under the private ordering regime.[16] The inherent opaqueness of the LBO and private equity model does not prevent this outcome.

---

13 See for the definitions: Michael Schillig, 'The Contribution of Law and Economics as a Method of Legal Reasoning in European Private Law' (Alphen aan den Rijn, The Netherlands) 17 European Review of Private Law 853, 860–61.

14 Pareto efficiency, which is an important concept in this thesis, because it shows under which conditions the GP and LP outcomes can be improved, means a scenario, where no other solution Pareto dominates it. Pareto dominance, on the other hand, means that there is no outcome that one party is better off, and the others are not worse off. See generally e.g.: Ronald Coase, 'The Nature of the Firm' (1937) 4 Economica 386.

15 While I recognise that the AIFMD is part of a broader legislative framework and also covers all other fund types, such as hedge funds, the findings of the Investment Game give insight into the proper scope of regulation at least in relation to private equity funds. Arguably, a number of the provisions of the AIFMD are more suitable in regulating hedge fund type of business. See e.g.: Payne, 'Private Equity and Its Regulation in Europe'.

16 The general game structure and idea is based on Oren Sussman's economic analysis of similar relationships discussed in Oxford First Principles of Financial Economics course: Notes and materials on the First Principles of Financial Economics, Oxford 2019.

This has implications on regulating management and operation of AIFMs[17] and AIFs (alternative investment funds), inducements,[18] conflict of interests management[19] and personal transactions of the management[20] as well as the upper managements supervisory obligations[21] under the AIFMD and the AIFM Delegated Regulation[22] (AIFMR).[23] What these rules have in common is that they regulate a number of the issues that the Investment Game seeks to solve under free-contracting regime. Extensive regulatory intervention has an effect on the game, which may lead to distortions in the incentive structure and, consequently, possible lower the utility of the market participants without commensurate benefits to the society. However, the findings are qualified if the level of undisclosed private benefits (of the managers or affiliated parties) cannot be determined *ex ante*. This is the case if there is no large-enough independent 'anchor' LP or a coherent LP group internalising enough private benefits from affecting the distribution of private benefits and affecting the fund terms. If the investor base is dispersed, will be difficult to overcome the opaqueness of the LBO structure and private benefits of the parties affiliated with the GP. However, the Investment Game enables, irrespective of a possible failure to affect the fund terms, an analysis of the level of undisclosed private benefits and effort levels. Therefore, the Investment Game also sets a basis for solving the game and assisting, through data analysis, with the question whether to invest in a particular fund or not.

---

17 Article 12 of the AIFMD and, mainly, articles 16–18 and 21–23 of the AIFMR. The main exclusion is UCITS funds that are retail funds covered by Directive 2009/65/EC of the European Parliament and of the Council of 13 July 2009 on the coordination of laws, regulations and administrative provisions relating to undertakings for collective investment in transferable securities 2009/65/EC. The UCITS Directive has been subject to several amendments, most Recently UCITS IV (EU) 2019/1160.

18 Article 13 and Schedule II of the AIFMD and Article 24 of the AIFMR.

19 Article 14 of the AIFMD and Section 2 of the AIFMR.

20 Article 63.

21 Mainly Articles 15 and 18 of the AIFMD and Articles 57and 61 of the AIFMR.

22 Commission Delegated Regulation (EU) No 231/2013 of 19 December 2012 supplementing Directive 2011/61/EU of the European Parliament and of the Council with regard to exemptions, general operating conditions, depositaries, leverage, transparency and supervision.

23 Although, the focus of the article is not jurisdiction-specific, I have limited the discussion for the purposes of conciseness to the relevant European Union Regulation. The AIFMD regulates a number of other material aspects of fund management in the EU such as depositories, valuation, incorporation requirements, reporting and disclosure obligations to the investors, authorities and the target companies. However, these are not as relevant with the Investment Game. The disclosure obligations naturally affect the GP-LP relationship, but these are not material to solving the game.

As a result, I argue that the fund investing challenges connected to the theoretical problems in Section 3 can be reduced with minimal regulatory intervention by giving the parties sufficient incentives to achieve Pareto improvements contractually rather than through extensive or 'one-size-for-all' regulation. This applies irrespective of the opacity of the underlying LBO financing structures. In relation to retail funds and widely dispersed investor base, a better alternative to regulatory intervention may be to require compliance with the contracting practice of the wholesale market instead.

1.3 *The Structure of the Paper*

I will first introduce in Section 2 some general features of private equity contracting and the parties relationships. In Section 3, I address the hidden information problem, the hidden action problem and the agency costs and how these materialise in private equity investing. The analysis is supported by a discussion of financial agency costs and strategic creditor actions. Section 3 concludes with the key propositions for the Investment Game.

Section 4 contains the structure of the Investment Game, the parameters, the potential outcomes for the parties, the unique equilibria and for the game dynamics of the Investment Game. Section 5 includes the conclusions.

2 Basic Structure of Private Equity Contracting

2.1 *Introduction*

Private equity funds are investment structures governed by a fund manager or a general partner managing a private equity fund, which is entirely, or almost entirely, funded by limited partners that are usually institutional investors.[24] Although the investor space is usually professional, some types of funds can be offered also to retail investors.[25] Fund management companies are invariably regulated entities subject supervision of national financial supervisory authorities.[26]

---

24 Steven N. Kaplan and Per Strömberg, 'Leveraged Buyouts and Private Equity' (2009) 23 Journal of Economic Perspectives 121, 123–24.

25 Such funds are subject to more stringent regulatory requirements.

26 For example, in the EU, fund management is a regulated activity (so-called alternative investment managers) within the EU under the AIFMD. Engaging in the business of investment management under the directive, requires licencing of the management company, i.e. so-called AIFM. Licensing enables the management company to offer fund units gross-border within the EU. However, more lenient registration obligations apply for funds that have less than €500 million (and if the redemption period is less than

Private equity funds are commonly structured as closed-end funds, albeit often with more than one closing, where the primary investors (LPs) are institutions, insurance companies, corporations and affluent family offices. Despite the fact that private equity funds can be set up in many legal forms, depending on the jurisdiction, the most common ways are to form the fund as a limited partnership or special limited partnership.[27] However, private equity funds are structured similarly in most jurisdictions.

The general partner and the investment manager are often established as limited liability companies. For certain liability and tax reasons the actual portfolio advisory may also be arranged through a separate advisory company that is in most jurisdictions subject to a separate licensing requirement.[28] Both are in practice owned by the private equity firm and its certain partners and managers.

The private equity fund and general acquisition and financing structure relevant to the analysis of the Investment Game is set out below in figure 1. There are three important relationships. The uppermost rectangle identifies the parties of the Investment Game. They are general partner, limited partners, advisory firm and the fund itself. 'Fund' refers to the entity the units of which are marketed to limited partners and which is primarily funded by their capital commitments. The parties' relationship is based primarily on a limited partnership agreement, subscription agreements and the disclosure documentation.

The second rectangle from the top sets out the relationship between the fund and the managers of the portfolio companies the fund holds. The fund will aim to align the interests of the managers with its own to deal with the managerial agency costs. The parties' relationships are governed by a

five years) under their management, or €100 million for levered funds. Management of certain funds offered to public (so-called UCITS funds) is subject to different EU level legislation. In comparison, e.g. in Singapore, Singapore fund management companies that carry out 'fund management' is required to have a capital markets services licence for the purposes of the fund management activity. If the total assets under management of the fund manager do not exceed S$250 million and if it has a maximum of 30 clients (the maximum of 15 of these clients can be funds or limited partnerships) the fund manager can opt to be registered instead of licensing. The fund manager can, however, avoid the licensing and registration obligation if it falls under one of the licensing exemptions, see Section 289 of the Singapore Securities and Futures Act.

27 There are also other variations, such as Singapore variable capital companies.

28 In the EU, the entity carrying out fund management activities is called an alternative investment manager and it needs to obtain a license to carry out its operations within the EU. Licenced AIFMs are, however, entitled to carry out cross-border fund management activities through the EU passporting regime.

management shareholder agreement, equity documentation and individual manager agreements.

The lowest rectangle sets out the relationship between a portfolio group (controlled by the fund) as a debtor and its creditors. The creditors' objective is to control strategic creditor actions arising in distress scenarios as well as financial agency costs faced by the creditors. These are important to the Investment Game because the structure of an LBO may lead to misalignment of the GP-LP interests higher up in the figure. The main documents governing this relationship are the facility agreements, bond indentures, security documents and the intercreditor agreement.[29]

The three relationships set out a 'risk-allocation space' of the fund, within which it is able to engage in value creation activities for the manager and the LPs. This space also constitutes the space for the asymmetric information and agency costs problems. Any legislation or regulation that aims to regulate such

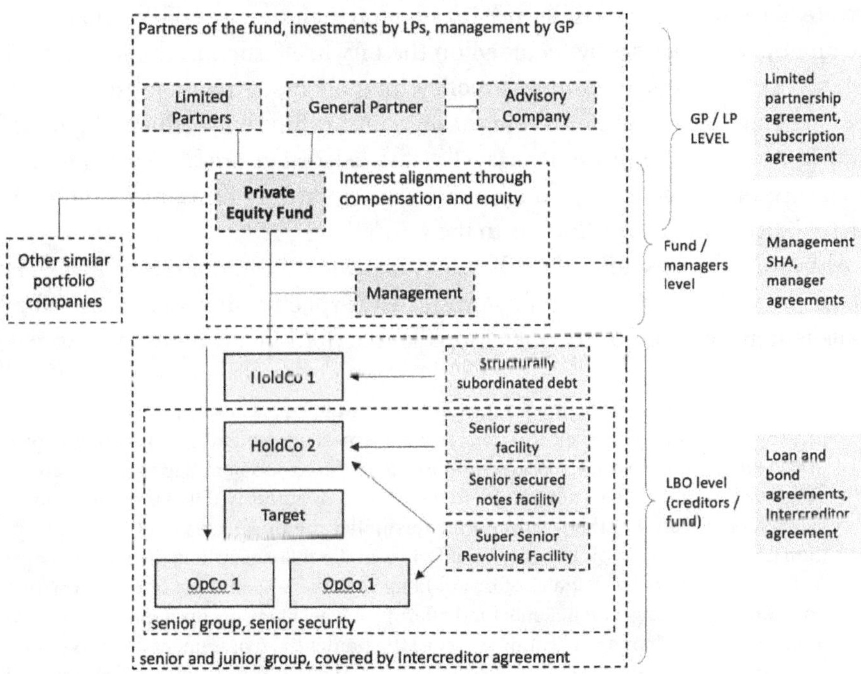

FIGURE 1 Private equity fund and acquisition structure

29 See for a theoretical and empirical analysis of the intercreditor agreements: Mika Lehtimaki, *Intercreditor agreement as a contractual solution to restructuring leveraged buyouts* (2020).

fund management activities will need to be mindful of the structure and operation of this risk allocation space. Consequently, it is important evaluate how the economic relationships between the above stakeholders are built in a free contracting environment before imposing regulatory requirements that necessarily affect the Pareto optimality of the risk allocation space. I will describe some aspects of the three relationships and the contracts governing these in more detail below.

2.2 *The GP-LP Contractual Framework*

2.2.1 General Framework

Limited partners (LPs) adhere to a limited partnership agreement and commit in a subscription agreement to pay a capped equity investment into the fund over its investment period.[30] Despite being often within the securities law exemptions in relation to prospectus obligation, it is commonplace that the GP or the management company provides potential investors with an extensive private placement memorandum.[31] It will often include some of the important documents not necessarily included on the LPA itself, such as the investment policy, the conflicts of interests policy, management team presentations, detailed rules on the use of leverage and relationships with affiliated parties, fund administration mechanics as well as the risk disclosures.[32] On-going fund disclosure occurs generally on an annual and quarterly basis, based on contractual disclosure commitments to the LPs.[33]

Although, the LPs adhere to the contracts with the same terms, investors often use 'side-letters' detailing any investor-specific deviations e.g. from management fee, disclosure obligations and certain investments.[34] However,

30 Kaplan and Strömberg, 'Leveraged Buyouts and Private Equity', 123–24.

31 In the EU, the relevant prospectus exemptions are most often offering of units only to professional investors or with consideration exceeding €100.000 per offering. In Singapore, fund itself normally does not require to be licensed or authorised if it is offered only to accredited or certain other types of investors under the prospectus publishing exemption under section 305 of the SSFA. For offerings under this exemption, the fund manager will only have to make a straight-forward filing with the MAS and to file an information memorandum along with it. Retail fund offerings attract a prospectus requirement, however, and will lead to the obligation to follow the prudential requirements of the SSFA.

32 Sam Kay: Private Equity Fund Structures in Chris Hale, Private Equity: A Transactional Analysis, Fourth Edition (4th edn, Globe Law and Business 2020) 47.

33 For example the AIFMD and the AIFMR require licensed fund management companies to make periodic reports and disclosure (AIFMD 24 art) to its supervisor as well as to its investors (AIFMD 23 art).

34 David T. Robinson and Berk A. Sensoy, 'Do Private Equity Fund Managers Earn Their Fees? Compensation, Ownership, and Cash Flow Performance' 26 The Review of Financial Studies 2760, 2780–81.

in those cases, the other LPs are often entitled to apply the same deviations, despite ones that relate e.g. to the size of the commitment, e.g. fee arrangements and seats in the investment committee.[35] The committed funds are called in the fund by the fund manager when making individual investments.[36] LPs cannot withdraw their commitments, except in exceptional circumstances and with a considerable discount, e.g. 30–50% or most of their investment.[37] Private equity funds have a pre-defined, often extendable, investment period and subsequent holding period, after which the fund is liquidated. Such funds are, therefore, likely to prefer capital structures with maturities within the duration of their fund to ensure they are not subject to a risk of liquidity or maturity transformation risk.[38]

2.2.2 The Limited Partnership Agreement

The most important provisions applying between the GPs and the LPs are included in the limited partnership agreement. Although such contractual terms are always heavily negotiated depending on the nature, desired risk level, management team, objectives, duration and the investment policy of the group, they are similarly structured in international transactions.

The first category of clauses in the LPA consists of the economic, i.e. commercial terms, which include the mechanics of the distribution of the funds income and assets, the management fee, operative and transaction fees, possible fee offsets the 'hurdle'-rate for the return to the LPs after return of the capital, the 'carry', i.e. relative share of the assets exceeding the LP capital return and the hurdle rate, and possible clawback of GP distributions in certain situations.[39]

The second category consists of the investor protection provisions, which include e.g. the rules for removal of the GP, key executive provisions, early termination, investment restrictions, borrowing restrictions, advisory committee

35 Sam Kay: Private Equity Fund Structures in Hale, *Private Equity: A Transactional Analysis, Fourth Edition* 50.

36 The call period is usually ca. 10 days, and a breach of the funding obligation will lead to severe penalties for a defaulting investor.

37 Sam Kay: Private Equity Fund Structures in Hale, *Private Equity: A Transactional Analysis, Fourth Edition* 56.

38 These risks are more pronounced in hedge fund investments, which usually have e.g. 30-day or other fixed redemption periods. The fact that private equity fund commitments are binding and subject to repayment only in very exceptional circumstances, means that they do not face material maturity or liquidity mismatch in their capital structure versus their investments. This also means that the need for bank-like capital and liquidity regulation is not as pressing with such funds.

39 See e.g. Kay in Hale, *Private Equity: A Transactional Analysis, Fourth Edition* 50–52.

provisions and certain limitations for starting successor funds. Importantly for the Investment Game analysis, the investor protection provisions also regulate fair and preferential treatment of the LPs, object of the fund, liability of the partners, conflict of interests, depositary clauses and indemnification provisions. It is fairly common to include some of these, e.g. the specific investment policies, conflicts policies and the like, in the private placement memoranda instead of the LPA.

The third category of clauses in the LPA are the operational provisions, which include administrative provisions relating to the fund units, their form, issuance and redemption, net asset value calculation, powers of the GP and their delegation, powers and decision mechanics of the general meetings and other meetings, representation and voting, as well as auditing, tax, liquidation of the fund and transfers of fund units.

The LPA clauses and the fund documentation form an extensive contractual regime which determines in detail the rights and obligations of the parties and any consequences for their breach. Despite this, and even though the clauses regulating conflicts of interests and general partner and manager operative and management obligations in the LPAS are extensive, the provisions concerning the effort put in by the management are often of general nature, vague and not subject to effective legal remedies should they be breached.[40] This is an important issue that will be pronounced in the Investment Game.

2.3 *Relationship with the Management*

One of the main mechanisms how private equity funds create value is by aligning the incentives of the managers of the acquired portfolio companies with their own incentives.[41] Two of the most strategies for achieving this are concentration of ownership in the portfolio firms along with efficient monitoring and bonding of the management. In order to deal with the management agency costs, funds align the incentives of the portfolio companies' management with their own usually by giving them an opportunity for a substantial upside through share ownership.[42]

40 It should be noted that the statutory and common law fiduciary duties that apply to the investment managers or in this case the advisory company and the management team are often very limited and often heavily qualified and limited in the limited partnership agreements.

41 Ulf Axelson, Per Strömberg and Michael S. Weisbach, 'Why Are Buyouts Levered? The Financial Structure of Private Equity Funds' (2009) LXIV Journal of Finance 1549, 1573.

42 Adam Orr: Equity Finance in Hale, *Private Equity: A Transactional Analysis, Fourth Edition* 64–70.

It should be noted here that the managers often get ordinary shares in the top holding company, whereas the private equity funds most likely hold subordinated loans and preferred equity in the top holding company.[43] This means that in practice the fund will be paid before the management and the management's equity holding will have value only after any such distributions. This also means that exceptional sale proceeds will lead to a very large upside for the management equity strip.[44]

2.4 *The Business: Leveraged Buy-outs*

LBOs are acquisitions of a company, or a group of companies carried out using significant amounts of various classes of indebtedness to meet the costs of the acquisition. LBOs are the primary way how private equity funds acquire target companies. Such financing structures often employ several holding and operating companies and layers of indebtedness.[45] The main reasons for such layering of debt and claims are the need to fix the priorities of various stakeholders, in respect to equity, debt and management, as well as structuring the acquisition group efficiently for tax purposes and for downstreaming the fund investment and management investments into the structure.[46] Furthermore, a multi-tiered holding-company structure may also enable better asset and debt partitioning for the fund and the ability for the secured creditors to enforce their security on an optimal level of the debtor group.

---

43 Ibid 66–68. See for general discussion on subordinated debt: Mika J. Lehtimaki, *Debt subordination in corporate liquidation* (2007).

44 Hale, *Private Equity: A Transactional Analysis, Fourth Edition* 64–66. For example, the funds often also subordinate the equity held by the managers to that of the private equity fund so that the managers are not compensated for the added value pari passu with the fund but only after reaching relatively high financial thresholds., Phalippou, 'Modifying Carried Interest To Do What It Is Said To Do' 3. However, in 'secondary' transactions where the old management invests a part of its sale proceeds into the new holding structure as a part of the 'institutional strip', they hold similar assets to those of the fund in relation to the reinvestment, See Adam Orr: Equity Finance in Hale, *Private Equity: A Transactional Analysis, Fourth Edition* 64–66.

45 See David Billington in Andrew Shutter, *A practitioner's guide to syndicated lending* (Andrew Shutter ed, Sweet & Maxwell: Thomson Reuters 2010) 86.

46 See concerning how LBOs generate value: Luc Renneboog and Cara Vansteenkiste, 'Leveraged Buyouts: A Survey of the Literature (March 9, 2017)'. CentER Paper Discussion Series No 2017-015, 4–13 and also Philip Wood, *Project finance, securitisations, subordinated debt* (2nd edn, Sweet & Maxwell 2007) 10–009.

LBOs are an example of the private equity funds' specialist capabilities in capital structuring and financing arrangements, which means that they are often able to take advantage also of more favourable credit markets and conditions.[47] This creates value arguably through lower cost of credit and more flexible financing agreements, i.e. the ability to incur additional debt without renegotiating the agreements.[48] The most important provisions regulating the LBO financing structure are found in the debt facilities agreement, bond terms, other debt documents and the intercreditor agreement, whereas the relevant theoretical problems here concern the risk of strategic creditor actions and financial agency costs.[49]

All of the above, i.e. the GP-LP dynamic, the GP-management relationship and the stakeholder conflicts in LBOs, lead to a set of theoretical questions that are relevant to the *structure* of the investment game. These are discussed in the following.

3 Investment Rationale and the Theoretical Questions

3.1 *Rationale in Investing and the Main Risks with Private Funds*

3.1.1 Introduction

From the perspective of the private equity fund, private contracting concerning the LP, creditor and management relationships results in a 'risk-allocation space' and value-creation opportunities for the fund.[50] Before analysing this risk-allocation space and the effects of the Investment Game and the other relationships on it, we will need to set out some aspects and rationale for

47 Ulf Axelson and others, 'Borrow Cheap, Buy High? The Determinants of Leverage and Pricing in Buyouts' 68 Journal of Finance 2223, 3 and 24. See also Andrey Malenko and Nadya Malenko, 'A theory of LBO activity based on repeated debt-equity conflicts' 117 Journal of Financial Economics 607. See concerning the use of collateralised debt obligations and loosening of debt covenants: See John Gilligan and Mike Wright, *Private Equity Demystified, An explanatory guide* (2nd edn, ICAEW Corporate Finance Faculty 2010) 2.4.6 and Matthew T. Billett and others, 'Bank Skin in the Game and Loan Contract Design: Evidence from Covenant-Lite Loans' 51 839. on the correlation between the CLO activity and contractual protections: Anil Shivdasani and Yihui Wang, 'Did Structured Credit Fuel the LBO Boom?' (2011) 66 Journal of Finance 66 1291.

48 Such negotiations and restructuring are costly.

49 See for an analysis of such costs and overcoming them in LBOs: Lehtimaki, *Intercreditor agreement as a contractual solution to restructuring leveraged buyouts.*

50 There are several ways how such private equity funds create value transactions and in the portfolio companies. In addition to finding operational efficiencies and growth, some of the most important ways are focusing of reducing shareholder-related agency costs, possible wealth transfers from creditors to equity, financial engineering, tax optimisation, dealing with undervaluation, takeover defences, and transaction structuring. See

investing in the private markets through funds. This will enable us to set out the *parameters* of the Investment Game.

Public markets are usually considered to be efficient, which means that they should reflect a fair market value of the securities. At least a part of this efficiency can be attributed to securities regulation and disclosure obligations.[51] Consequently, the additional costs of deploying capital in such markets is often lower than in the private markets.[52] Private equity markets are, on the other hand, more less transparent, which is likely to lead to less efficiency. This means that it may be difficult to distinguish feasible investments from bad ones.[53]

Because of these difficulties, and considering significant risks of information asymmetries, investors are likely to want to avoid the 'negative alpha'[54] in making their investment decisions in the markets of unlisted securities. Therefore, they are likely to use financial intermediaries to act on their behalf, to carry out the financial and operative analysis and to align the interests of the companies' management to that with the fund.[55] The problems that the investors need to deal with in relation to such information asymmetries are two-fold.

3.1.2 Hidden Information and Hidden Action Problems

The first of these is the problem of adverse selection, i.e. the question of hidden information.[56] It is based on 'opaqueness' of certain assets traded on the markets. If there is no credible cost-effective way of conveying the true value and qualities of the assets to the markets, differentiation between 'good' and the 'bad' assets becomes impossible.[57] This, in turn will drive the prices to an equilibrium that is lower, at least, for the good products than it were if the

generally on the literature dealing with some of these claimed value creation mechanisms: Renneboog and Vansteenkiste, 'Leveraged Buyouts: A Survey of the Literature (March 9, 2017)'. 5–13.

51 Ludovic Phalippou, *The Future of Private Markets* (*June 30, 2018*) (Available at SSRN: https://ssrn.com/abstract=3170928 2018) 2.

52 Ibid.

53 As emphasized by Sahlman (1990), Kaplan and Strömberg (2001, 2004), and Cumming (2005a, 2005b, 2006), the riskiness of PE investments is increased by the high asymmetric information and agency problems (i.e., effort problems, information problems, conflict of interests, free-riding, lock-up situations).

54 The terms negative alpha here refers to the possible excess return delivered by the relevant investment strategy over the relevant benchmark index.

55 See generally Ludovic Phalippou, 'The Future of Private Markets (June 30, 2018)' Available at SSRN: https://ssrncom/abstract=3170928 1–3.

56 George A. Akerlof, *The market for "lemons": quality uncertainty and the market mechanism* (1970).

57 See for the original description: ibid.

purchasers had sufficient information for proper valuation.[58] If the owners of good assets do not have credible and cost effective ways of signalling the true qualities to the markets, they will either withdraw from the market or lower the price to the level of the bad assets.[59] Surely, the owners of bad assets have no incentive for disclosing the true qualities of their assets. The logic for price-setting under the adverse selection problem is visualised in the below figures 2a and 2b. As can be seen from the figure the adverse selection problem is an *equilibrium problem*.

In the Investment Game the 'opaque' assets are the fund units, and the LBO target companies. As described above, institutional investors seek to deal with the opaqueness of investing in private companies and the adverse selection M&A pricing by using financial intermediaries that are capable of overcoming these problems more cost-effectively: by sophisticated acquisition analysis, deal terms and financial and incentivisation structures. Use of intermediaries such as private equity funds, is therefore beneficial for the investors because it overcomes the problem of adverse selection, at least up to the level where the marginal cost of using the intermediary is less than the cost of dealing with the adverse selection problem by itself.

When we analyse the rationale for using private equity funds to overcome the hidden information problem, it appears counter-intuitive that e.g. under

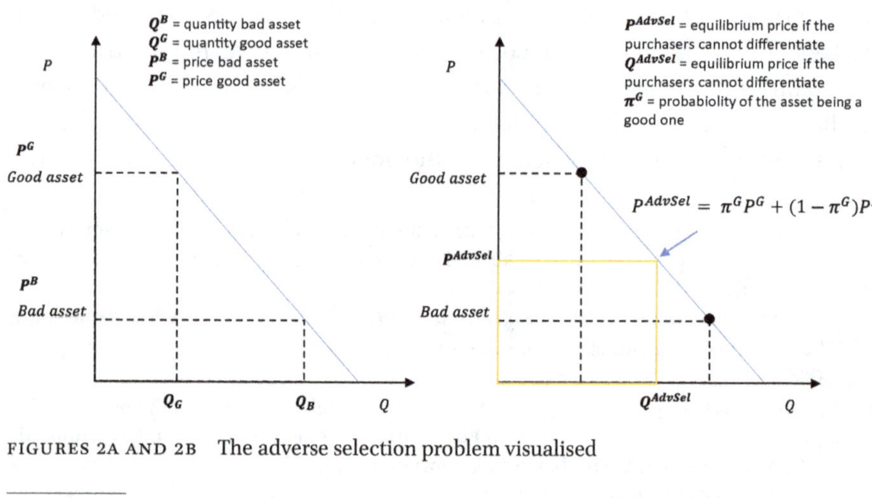

FIGURES 2A AND 2B The adverse selection problem visualised

58 See for a classic analysis on the effects of the information asymmetry on the capital structure of firms and the 'pecking order' of financing instruments: Stewart C. Myers and Nicholas S. Majluf, *Corporate Financing and Investment Decisions When Firms Have Information That Investors Do Not Have* (National Bureau of Economic Research 1984).

59 See generally Akerlof, *The market for "lemons": quality uncertainty and the market mechanism.*

the AIFMD fund managers need to follow sufficient due diligence policy and standards in selecting and executing investments for and on behalf of AIFs in light of the AIF's investment policy.[60] The due diligence obligations are broader if the investment concerns low-liquidity assets (such as private equity investments).[61] The obligations include preparation of a business plan, evaluation of the investment risks from the perspective of the available resources, market and interest factors and e.g. execute measures to ensure prudent management of low-liquidity investment's risks prior to the investment. Although, this requirement does not directly affect the structure of the Investment Game, it has a connection to its assumptions.

From the perspective of the Investment Game, the due diligence requirement is redundant, because it addresses the same problem already solved by the economic structure of a private equity fund and the GP-LP relationship. This is because, due to the opaqueness of private investments, LPs use financial intermediaries specifically to overcome the hidden information problem, which is also the main objective of regulating due diligence obligations.[62]

As for the private equity funds themselves, the nature of adverse selection problem is of a different form. When a fund issues fund units, it does not usually have any investment made. There is only the fund structure, management team, key persons, their track record and a possible investment into the fund.[63] None of these, even the track record, is necessarily a factor which would lead to misinformation in the same sense as with M&A transactions. Disclosure does not in that case resolve the credibility problem of such information. However, disclosure of the track record of the management team is surely rational from the perspective of another information asymmetry problem, the 'hidden effort' problem.

The hidden effort problem is material for solving the Investment Game because, instead of possible misleading information about the value of the portfolio companies, at the moment of committing their capital, the LPs can only make estimations of the success of the fund. One of the most central factors in this is the level of effort given by the GP and the management team to the funds. The hidden effort problem materialises if the fund managers have no credible way of committing to a high level of effort.[64] In addition, they have

60 Article 15, subsection 3 of the AIFMD.

61 Articles 18 and 19 of the AIFMR.

62 See section 3.1.2.

63 Such a commitment is likely to be within ca. 1–4% LP of the fund investments.

64 As discussed in Section 4, I have assumed in the Investment Game that high effort less the cost involved leads to a better result for the fund, provided that exogenous factors or the compensation structure do not disrupt this assumption.

a very high opportunity cost for committing a majority of their time to the fund e.g. for the next 10 years. Also, due to strong competitive environment value creation of the fund is strongly correlated with the skill and effort of the team in acquisitions, structuring, financing, negotiations and exit strategies as well as bringing in the best possible people to manage the portfolio companies and incentivising them properly.

Although it would appear hard to analyse the effects of the management effort *ex ante* on the success of the fund for investment and valuation purposes, the LPs are able to take an informed guess of the level of effort if they are able to evaluate the correlation between the level of effort and fund success and the private benefits the GP and its management obtains from the operation of the fund. Assuming that the fund management acts rationally, the proper effort level can be ensured with a proper incentivisation structure. Unlike the hidden information problem, the hidden effort problem is a *maximisation problem*, i.e. not solved directly e.g. by disclosure obligations but by promoting optimal behaviour by the fund manager.[65] Solving the hidden effort problem is material for the Investment Game.

3.1.3 The Statutory Perspective on Conflicts of Interest

The AIFM and the AIFMR as well as their delegated regulations contain extensive provisions dealing with the fund managers and other persons that have decision-making or supervisory powers in the AIFMs business. This is understandable because for example private equity and hedge funds invest in inherently opaque and complex transactions. First, the AIFMD requires the fund manager to identify conflicts of interests arising between inter alia itself, management, affiliated parties, the fund, LPs, other managed funds and their investors. This is connected to a conflicts policy the AIFM is obligated to prepare under the AIFMR, which will also have to take into account broader financial group the AIFM belongs to.[66]

Secondly, the fund manager needs to maintain and use effective organisational and management arrangements to acknowledge, prevent, control and supervise conflicts of interest. This means ensuring that the persons active in transactions that may result in conflicts act sufficiently independently. Most importantly, the AIFMR requires the AIFM to evaluate whether itself, its management or affiliated persons may likely receive financial benefits or avoid

65 Institutional investors are able to resort to sophisticated financial databases and investment analysis that they can utilise in the portfolio analysis for investment and diversification purposes. However, such an analysis becomes even more interesting and insightful once we are able to combine such data with the Investment Game equilibria and outcome maximisation problems.

66 Article 14 of the AIFMD and Articles 30–37 of the AIFMR.

financial loss at the expense of the fund or its investors and whether it receives a benefit deviating from the interests of the fund investors. If the conflicts can be eliminated, they will have to be disclosed to the LPs.

However, it is important to note that the fund manager already has an economic incentive to deal with the conflict of interests problem, an agency costs issue. The reason is that the LPs assume the risk of existence of such conflicts, given the opaqueness, and will price their expectations in their investment decision. Therefore, the funds should have adequate incentives to disclose and manage conflict scenarios, provided the LPs have sufficient negotiating leverage, whether alone or collectively. However, for example with fund offered to retail investors, the LPs are unlikely to have the ability to affect the terms and the pricing. Therefore, extensive EU level regulation is understandable in retail fund offerings.

3.1.4 The Rationale of the GP for Using Equity Funding

As discussed in Section 3.1.1 above, it can be argued that LPs have an incentive for using financial intermediaries to reduce the negative alpha. How about GPs? If we assume that they are better in defusing e.g. the adverse selection problem, would they not be able to utilise maximum fund leverage to finance the acquisitions also on the fund level instead of seeking more expensive private equity for the fund? Although the question of cost of equity versus debt in funds cannot be analysed here, we should note two reasons why the GP will prefer equity on the fund level.

First, the use of equity instead of debt lowers the insolvency risk on the fund level to a minimum. All of the debt is usually incurred on the portfolio company level, so equity financing shields the fund and the GP from a systematic fund-wide insolvency risk.[67] The second reason is connected to different approaches to risk the GP and the LPs of investing in equity. On a general level, we can assume that the benefits obtained by both parties concern effective allocation of this risk. From the GPs perspective offering of equity, or in this case LP units in the fund, is equivalent to distributing the idiosyncratic risk

67 It should be noted that it is possible to leverage the fund on the 'fund level' instead. Most private equity funds use leverage to bridge the equity capital calls and the payment obligations of their target acquisitions. However, it is also possible to leverage the fund more extensively on that level. Such scenarios are often subject to stricter regulatory rules. E.g. in the EU fund level leverage results in a lower mandatory authorisation regime for the management company (100m euros) and to a stricter disclosure regime. However, Portfolio level-leverage disclosure is often also regulated, but like in the EU, it relates to systemic effect of use of high leverage and disclosure obligations concerning the use of leverage.

inherent in the portfolio companies to the LPs.[68] They often hold, due to their institutional nature, diversified portfolios of securities and investment assets, which means that analysis they are able to structure, e.g. under the CAPM[69] analysis, a risk-neutral portfolio or a portfolio at a desired risk level.

The above means that LPs can bear a large portion of the idiosyncratic risk with a lower cost. This in turn results in a likelihood of the LPs are likely putting a higher value to the fund units than the GP, being willing to pay a higher price for them.[70] Such a strategy will in turn enable the GP to take on higher risk or higher profit projects and also to receive higher private benefits from the fund and portfolio companies. This is often seen in the acquisition structures, which, unlike the fund level, utilises considerable financial leverage.

Therefore, the bankruptcy risk is effectively pushed down from the fund on the portfolio level. This way the GP can also benefit from its specialist financial structuring skills while effecting optimal bankruptcy risk allocation to the creditor base. The negative aspect of being able to take higher risks on both the fund and the portfolio level are, however, the rising agency costs and risk of moral hazard in the structure.[71]

These risks can be controlled on two levels. First of all, the GP will need to deal with the agency costs of the managers of the portfolio companies. Secondly, the GP will need to convince the LPs, or ensure the same contractually, that the agency costs caused by the GPs' and their affiliates' incentives lower in the company structure are not so high as to prohibit LPs' fund investments or raise the LPs required rate of return on an unfeasible level.

3.2 *The Agency Costs*

3.2.1 Introduction

The above problems concerning information asymmetries are closely connected to so-called management agency costs, which are inherent in all structures utilising financial intermediaries.[72]

---

68 See on the distribution on the idiosyncratic risk between asset managers and investors: Joost Driessen, Tse-Chun Lin and Ludovic Phalippou, *A New Method to Estimate Risk and Return of Non-traded Assets from Cash Flows: The Case of Private Equity Funds (February 14, 2011)* (Journal of Financial and Quantitative Analysis (JFQA), Forthcoming, EFA 2007 Ljubljana Meetings Paper, AFA 2008 New Orleans Meetings Paper, Swedish Institute for Financial Research Conference on The Economics of the Private Equity Market).

69 Capital Asset Pricing Model.

70 See for a more general description: James Spindler, 'How Private Is Private Equity?' (Washington) 32 Regulation 38, 39.

71 Ibid.

72 Michael C. Jensen and William H. Meckling, *Theory of the firm: managerial behavior, agency costs and ownership structure* (1976) 308–10. Such agency costs arise in connection

Such agency costs arise, on the one hand, between the LPs and the GP and, on the other hand, between the GP and the managers of the portfolio companies that the fund acquires. The nature of the agency costs in these two relationships is the same, but the decision-making structures are different.[73]

3.2.2 The Basic Dilemma Faced by Owners and Managers

In a manager-owned company, the utility of the manager deriving from a firm is based not only on the financial returns derived from the company but also of 'various non-pecuniary benefits' associated with the position.[74] However, the manager also bears all of the costs of such benefits. A sale of a portion of the equity changes the incentives of the shareholders because, after such a sale, the manager-shareholder bears only partially the cost of the non-pecuniary benefits.[75]

However, in efficient markets, the other shareholders are able to anticipate these wealth effects, which are reflected in the price of the firm's securities. Therefore, a manager selling the shares is likely to bear the effects of the agency costs and, consequently be incentivised to reduce them by granting increased monitoring and bonding rights to the shareholders.[76] The divergence of the manager's decisions from the decisions maximizing the investor's welfare is the sum of the investor's monitoring expenditures, bonding expenditures by the manager and the 'residual loss'.[77]

The benefits of concentrated share ownership implies that an owner-manager would benefit from acquiring the entire share capital of the firm with debt, eliminating the manager-shareholder conflict. In general, the use of debt may be preferable to a sale of equity if the agency costs of debt are less than the loss of wealth (utility) resulting from the equity sale.[78]

---

with any business activity that involves the separation of ownership and management or control of an asset, i.e. between a principal and an agent. This is also true for private equity investments because there will inevitably arise situations where the objectives of the fund managers and the investors differ, e.g. due to different expectations of a proper exit time, the need to display the investments in different light or due to different compensation structures of the parties.

73 In addition to the management agency problem, also the creditors of the portfolio companies may face agency costs in the form of financial agency costs. Although to a lesser extent than the management agency costs, also the financial agency costs affect the parties' incentive structures and expectation in the Investment Game.

74 Jensen and Meckling, *Theory of the firm: managerial behavior, agency costs and ownership structure* 312.

75 Ibid.

76 Ibid, especially 313–19.

77 Ibid 308.

78 Ibid 333–37.

Resolution of these types of management agency costs problems is characteristic to private equity portfolio investments, where the fund in effect acquires almost all of the equity of the company with debt and equity. The fund will incentivise the management of the company with equity compensation backed by monitoring and control clauses used in the shareholders' agreements of the holding companies. This means that the fund aims to align the incentives of the portfolio management fully with its own incentives.

Therefore, the solutions to the management agency costs problem would appear to be beneficial not only for the GP but also for the LPs. As a matter of a fact, the ability to effect such an incentive alignment by the fund is one of the reasons for the LPs to use financial intermediaries in private company investments.[79]

3.2.3 Statutory Perspective on Compensation Policies

Under the AIFMD, fund managers need to have an upper management compensation policy that supports its risk management policy, and which does not promote risk taking on behalf of the fund that is inconsistent with the funds' risk profile or their rules.[80] The compensation policy should also be aligned with the objectives of the fund and its investors as well as include measures to reduce conflicts of interest between the fund managers and the investors.[81]

ESMA has issued guidelines regulating performance fees and sound remuneration policies under the AIFMD.[82] However, the guidelines do not apply e.g. to private equity fund managers in connection with the Investment Game-type of a scenario. However, such fund managers will still need to comply with the compensation and inducement policy set out in Schedule III of the AIFMD.

This means that the compensation policy should be reviewed by the management body at least annually. The AIFMD requires setting up of a relatively independent compensation board for fund managers of substantial size or importance. This ensures that the compensation policies are adopted and implemented subject to supervision from parties whose compensation is not directly connected to those of the persons handling the management, risk or portfolio management of the fund. The compensation policy rules apply in practice to all upper management, portfolio managers, compliance and risk management functions material for the fund manager's business or organisation.[83]

---

79 Large institutional investors seldom have teams to carry out such incentivisation or monitoring of the target firms.

80 Schedule II of the AIFMD.

81 See especially Article 13 of the AIFMD.

82 ESMA Guidelines on performance fees in UCITS and certain types of AIFS, ESMA34-39-992, 5/11/2020.

83 Ibid.

The AIFMD Compensation Schedule requires that revenue or profit-based compensation depends on the individual performance of the relevant person, the results of the particular fund, the total results of the fund manager covering both financial and other factors. As a rule, the evaluation should be based on the fund's multi-year life-cycle noting the redemption policy of the fund. In practice, because redemptions are not allowed in private equity funds, the life-cycle refers to the length of the investment and exit periods.

As a main rule, it is required that at least 50 percent of variable compensation is paid out as shares, fund units or other non-cash items. National authorities may impose additional requirements on the type of such compensation to ensure the payments align the fund manager's incentives with those of the LPs. A significant portion, at least 40 percent of the variable compensation part should be deferred over the life of the fund, the minimum of three to five years. For particularly large variable fees, the deferred portion should be increased to 60 percent. Any payments are conditional on them being sustainable from the financial perspective of the fund and the right to receive such payments should be reduced to deal with the possible worse financial performance of the fund. This means that the compensation mechanics 'internal' to the fund and the fund manager are strictly regulated and required to correspond to the duration of the fund investment.

3.3 *Management Agency Costs and Asymmetric Information Problems*

The nature of the agency costs in the GP-LP relationship stems from the same theoretical basis as between the fund and the directors of the portfolio companies. However, agency costs emerge between the GP and the LPs in a different way. Whereas in relation to the portfolio companies, the fund holds almost all of the shares, monitors the company and has devised a compensation structure ensuring maximum alignment of interests, the LPs do not have extensive control rights and remedies against the GP.[84] Also, the investment periods of private equity funds are long and fund disclosure or the manager's obligations may not be supported by sufficient remedies. This makes some of the mechanisms for controlling the management agency costs mechanisms inefficient.

However, for example Brown, Harris, Jenkinson and Kaplan note that, although there are important agency conflicts at work in private equity contracts, on average limited partnership agreements are alert to these conflicts and seek to align the LPs and the GPs incentives. They refer mainly to the fee

84 See concerning possible mechanisms: Ronald J. Gilson, 'Engineering a Venture Capital Market: Lessons from the American Experience' 55 Stanford Law Review 1067 and Lin Lin, 'Engineering a Venture Capital Market: Lessons from China' 30 Columbia Journal of Asian Law 160.

and profit related questions and consider that the relative statistical outperformance of private equity funds compared to the peers evidence this.[85] This is true and agency costs can indeed be controlled, or conversely worsened, by the compensation mechanisms of the GP that often include a management fee and a so-called carried interest component.[86] However, the effectiveness of the compensation solutions used in the LPAs is, by no means, clear.[87]

It is possible to try to control these costs e.g. by restricting offering of the funds to qualified investors,[88] through disclosure and through market-based measures, such as monitoring of fund performance, and by dividing investments into subsequent closings to monitor the performance of the fund managers as well as using performance-based compensation of the GPs.[89]

However, such solutions suffer from several deficiencies. First, depending on the size of the investor-base, there may not be large-enough a limited partner who would be able to internalise enough benefits from the monitoring. Secondly, one of the main reasons for using private equity structures from the point of view of the LPs is to access better alpha, investment and capital structuring expertise the LP may not possess and to allocate the decision-making to external managers for time and resource-saving purposes.[90]

Thirdly, even when monitoring would be justified, a large LP may not be incentivised to do so, if it has better own resources to monitor the fund or deal with the complexity of the documentation through more qualified legal support or if it can negotiate co-investment rights along with the fund, not enjoyed by the smaller LPs. Therefore, the rights of the LPs may not be aligned even if general monitoring by the LPs were seen as cost-effective. These concerns are connected to the difficulties in measuring funds' performance because the

85 Greg Brown and others, 'Private Equity: Accomplishments and Challenges' 32 Journal of Applied Corporate Finance 8, 18. See also for a very critical analysis: Ludovic Phalippou, *An Inconvenient Fact: Private Equity Returns & The Billionaire Factory (June 10, 2020)* (University of Oxford, Said Business School, Working Paper 2020).

86 See generally of various techniques: Gilson, 'Engineering a Venture Capital Market: Lessons from the American Experience', 1087–90.

87 For example, Phalippou has argued that the private market's attractiveness is based on magnitude of agency costs and the mitigants, i.e. the fund manager's alpha and fees, and the efficiency of the private fund market, Phalippou, *The Future of Private Markets (June 30, 2018)* 2.

88 See Section 2.2.3.

89 See e.g. ILPA, *ILPA Principles 3.0: Fostering Transparency, Governance and Alignment of Interests for General and Limited Partners* 10–16.

90 However, the costs connected to monitoring may not be a material factor, because private equity funds do in reality engage in extensive disclosure to the LPs, see e.g. Phalippou, *The Future of Private Markets (June 30, 2018)* 3.

fund commitments are for long-term, invariably without a put option or a right to terminate the limited partner's obligation to pay the agreed upon subscription amount.[91]

A more extensive form of monitoring is the ability to include corporate governance rules and fiduciary obligations into limited partnership agreements (LPAs) protecting the LPs against agency costs and moral hazard.[92] This may prove to be a difficult strategy for a number of reasons. First, under limited partnership legislation and relevant tax law of a number of jurisdictions, the ability of the LPs to make decisions in fund investments and matters may lead to loss of limited liability of the LPs and possible loss of beneficial tax treatment. Secondly, there is the question of remedies and consequences flowing from either breach of the disclosure rules, fiduciary obligations and breaches of conflict rules.[93] LPAs do not generally include substantive damages or termination clauses or regulation making possible to change the general partner of the fund other than is grave breaches of its statutory or contractual obligations.[94] In general, LPAs provide little tangible protections for the LPs against agency costs and moral hazard risk. Such agreements usually contain extensive clauses addressing potential conflicts of interest, but from the agency costs perspective these seldom provide any remedies to the LPs but rather deal with the internal procedures of the private equity group for addressing such questions.

This leaves us with external regulation, specific contractual protections and the structuring of the compensation mechanism is a way that aligns the incentives of the limited partners and the general partners in most relevant situations and limits the distorting effects of private benefits received by the fund

91 Sale of LP interests is always restricted, and breach of capital contribution obligations will usually lead to loss of the existing investment through redemption with a steep discount (e.g. 30% or 50% of the nominal value of its investment); See generally of the limited remedies: Spindler, 'How Private Is Private Equity?' 42–43. It should be noted that some of the contractual protections, such as transfer of the GP status to a new entity upon fraudulent actions or departure of the key persons, are more structural matter, not directly addressing the economic risk for agency costs or moral hazard concerns.

92 Investing in a private equity fund also entails a number of other agreements, such as a subscription agreement, possible side letter agreements and e.g. Co-investment agreements. See generally about the empirical literature on GPs fees relative to the net fees of the LPs received from the funds: Brown and others, 'Private Equity: Accomplishments and Challenges', 17–18.

93 See for the effect of lack of fiduciary duties in fund management: Chester Matthias Tan, 'Fiduciary Duties in the Private Equity and Venture Capital World' 4 International Comparative Jurisprudence 66.

94 Sam Kay: Private Equity Fund Structures in Hale, *Private Equity: A Transactional Analysis, Fourth Edition* 52–53.

manager. The rationale for the use of regulation instead of relying on contractual solutions is often said to be the impossibility to write 'complete contracts' regulating fund operations, protection of retail investors and the difficulty to resolve multi-layered agency conflicts.[95] There are two aspects to this: prevention of fraud and extensive disclosure regulation.

First of all, it should be noted that the fund managers will need to have a fraud prevention and management policy under the AIFMD.[96, 97] The rationale is clear. Actual LPAs contain few rules for dealing with fraud-related questions, except for the right to have the AIFM removed as a GP in certain situations.[98] However, the lack of legal remedies in the AIFMD itself means that a mandatory fraud prevention policy serves in practise disclosure and regulatory supervision purposes.[99] The Disclosure requirement is likely to arise in a litigation should the policy be incorporated into the LPA as a schedule, leading to potential breach of contract remedy under national law.[100]

Secondly, fund managers cannot charge unreasonable fees from their investors.[101] The prohibition of excessive fees deals directly with the fee structure of the fund and the AIFM. It is also one of the main aspects of the commercial provisions of LPAs and constitute primary variables of the Investment Game. At first sight, the provision may seem feasible, but it raises the question of appropriate fees the LPs approve to incentivise the GP to put high effort into management of the fund. Thirdly, we can argue, at least in relation to the information asymmetry problem, that alignment with the securities

---

95 See for a summary of the literature of the problem in private equity: Ludovic Phalippou, Christian Rauch and Marc Umber, 'Private equity portfolio company fees' 129 Journal of financial economics 559, 560. See for an empirical rebuttal of the incomplete contracting claim: Lehtimaki, *Intercreditor agreement as a contractual solution to restructuring leveraged buyouts* Parts C–D.

96 Article 12 (b) and (e) of the AIFMD.

97 Article 17.

98 Sam Kay: Private Equity Fund Structures in Hale, *Private Equity: A Transactional Analysis, Fourth Edition* 52–3.

99 See for the nature of sanctions for breach of AIFMD: Mariia Domina Repiquet, 'A Failed Attempt to Protect Hedge Fund Investors? An Inquiry into the Alternative Investment Fund Managers Directive' 12 Liberty University law review, 506–7. However, the disclosure requirement is likely to arise in a litigation should the policy be incorporated into the LPA as a schedule, leading to potential breach of contract remedy under national law.

100 See for the interplay between the private and statutory law remedies: ibid, 507–12. Repiquet points out that the AIFMD fails to provide sufficient protection to the fund investors through conduct of business rules. She notes that this results primarily from the lack of adequate remedies for the breach of the directive's obligations.

101 Article 17,2 of the AIFMR.

regulation of the public markets and more extensive fund regulation help to deal with the incentive alignment problem. However, there are several reasons for not extending the securities law obligations to private equity. E.g. a type of a disclosure rule leading to strict or severe liability for the GP for misstatements and omission to pay back the investments in full or in part may frustrate the very objective of optimal risk allocation between the GP and the LPs the structure was intended to achieve.[102] As we will see in Section 4, extension of securities law disclosure rules and more extensive fund regulation may not be a feasible strategy and that private contracting may achieve most of the objectives.

3.4 *Financial Agency Costs and Strategic Creditor Actions in LBOs*

3.4.1 Introduction

The hidden effort problem and the management agency costs provide a basis for analysis of the Investment Game. However, 'shifting the' leverage down the fund acquisition means that the Investment Game will have to consider possible financial agency costs faced by the creditors of the portfolio companies in relation to the debtor group and other creditors. The strategy of the fund to deal with these problems affects its economic incentives 'higher up' in the Investment Game.

Managing financial risk and restructuring distressed portfolio companies are some of the core competencies of private equity funds.[103] Some of these techniques lead to a heightened risk of financial agency costs in relation to portfolio companies acquired through leveraged buy-out transactions.[104] Perhaps

---

102 See Spindler, 'How Private Is Private Equity?' 40.

103 Brown and others, 'Private Equity: Accomplishments and Challenges', 11. See also Peter Morris and Ludovic Phalippou, 'Thirty years after Jensen's prediction: is private equity a superior form of ownership?' [Oxford University Press] 36 Oxford Review of Economic Policy, 304.

104 Also, e.g. Armour & Frisby have noted that the use of debt-related incentives, typical to private equity investments, can lead to material agency costs of debt, J. Armour and S. Frisby, 'Rethinking Receivership' (2001) 21 Oxford Journal of Legal Studies 73 80–82. On the other hand, Armour, Hertig and Kanda have argued that creditors face agency problems both *ex ante* and *ex post* entering into financing arrangements. First, they note that creditors face the risk of the debtor misrepresenting the value or title to the assets *ex ante*. Secondly, the creditors face the risk of the debtor transferring the assets of the debtor outside the corporate entity (*asset dilution*), by increasing the riskiness of the debtor's business (*asset substitution*), and by subsequently increasing the borrowing of the group (*debt dilution*), Armour, Hertig and Kanda in Reinier H. Kraakman and others, *The anatomy of corporate law: a comparative and functional approach* (Third edn, Oxford University Press 2017) 111–12 and 127–128.

the most obvious negative aspects of high leverage concern the owner-manager's (with limited equity exposure) incentives to engage in high-risk activities despite their low probability of success.[105] The effects on the Investment Game are two-fold.

First, although the use of high leverage has a disciplining effect on the portfolio company management, higher leverage increases the financial riskiness of the investment and the LPs encounter 'opaqueness' on the level of LBO financing.[106] The majority of the financial risk is borne, first, by the portfolio company creditors and, secondly, by the LPs (having provided almost all of the remaining capital for the initial acquisition). Although, the GP does not receive any profit should a portfolio company fail, it carries a smaller financial risk for such failure and the downside risk is countered by the fact that the GP and its affiliated entities may have collected substantial transaction and management fees as of the acquisition of a particular portfolio company.

The second effect of high leverage on the Investment Game relates to the LBO contractual regime. Sophisticated creditors expect existence of financial agency costs, and they seek protection against these risks e.g. by the use of covenants and monitoring rights in debt documents. In addition to these, the creditors also face the risk of creditors engaging in distress scenarios in hold-out and hold-up behaviour. In order for the controlling creditor group to capture the group going concern value in a portfolio company distress scenario, they need to be able to control the enforcement and sale of the debtor's assets *ex post*, to be able to maximise any going concern surplus of the debtor group. As a result, the debtor group and the fund have an incentive to offer its

105 Renneboog and Vansteenkiste note that 'wealth transfers from bondholders' are a source of shareholder-creditor incentive conflict and note that such wealth transfers can occur by means of increasing the riskiness of the firm's projects, dividends and other distributions and issuance of new or additional debt having either the same or better seniority than the existing indebtedness, Renneboog and Vansteenkiste, 'Leveraged Buyouts: A Survey of the Literature (March 9, 2017)'. 8. However, it is not evident that the strong interest alignment between the private equity funds and the portfolio company managers always leads to financial agency costs, especially between the managers and the creditors. For example, Sarah Paterson has argued that private equity fund transactions may lead to incentives of the management to support the creditors' restructuring plans instead of aligning with the fund. This may be the case even if there is residual value in the company, Sarah Paterson, 'The Paradox of Alignment: Agency Problems and Debt Restructuring' 17 European Business Organization Law Review 497 511. This is a difficult question because it involves leading with the agency costs problem on multiple levels, and which cannot be answered thoroughly in this thesis.

106 Investment performance and portfolio company disclosure seldom extends to such matters.

creditors clauses to enable group-wide enforcement and payment restrictions, group-wide asset disposals and releases of claims and security on a group-wide basis. Creditors of a same class control strategic creditor actions in the facility agreements by majority decision-making provisions, e.g. concerning acceleration of indebtedness, waivers and enforcement as well as through pro-rata distribution and turnover clauses.[107] Between different creditor groups, this can be achieved e.g. by intercreditor agreements,[108] which are in fact invariable used in private equity financing arrangements.[109] Dealing contractually with the agency costs and strategic creditor actions is likely to lower the cost of capital for the firm.[110]

In order to counter such extensive priority, control and enforcement provisions of the intercreditor agreements, private equity funds often negotiate extensive refinancing and incremental financing clauses into the financing documentation to retain maximum capital flexibility both when refinancing the group, increasing financing and for ensuring liquidity in a distress scenario. Such flexibility increases the bargaining leverage of the fund against the creditor-base.[111]

---

107 See generally: David Billington, 'Syndicated lending' in Andrew Shutter (ed), *A practitioner's guide to syndicated lending* (Second edn, Sweet & Maxwell 2017).

108 See for the underlying argumentation: Michael S. Knoll, *The Modigliani-Miller Theorem at 60: The Long-Overlooked Legal Applications of Finance's Foundational Theorem (October 11, 2017)*. (U of Penn, Inst for Law & Econ Research Paper No 17–43. Available at SSRN: https://ssrn.com/abstract=3053953 2017) (n 61). Also, according to Haugen and Senbet, the inclusion of contractual terms dealing with the risks of strategic creditor action should be costless in well-functioning capital markets and that such terms should be able to 'prevent free riders from impeding informal reorganisation of the capital structure', RA Haugen and LA Senbet, 'Bankruptcy and Agency Costs: Their Significance to the Theory of Optimal Capital Structure' (1988) 23 Journal of Financial and Quantitative Analysis 27 30.

109 Such agreements govern e.g. highest-ranking creditor group control rights, standstill clauses, *pro rata* distribution and turnover provisions as well as enforcement, sale and restructuring mechanisms. It should be noted that intercreditor agreements are one tool for the stakeholders in relation to the debtor group distress scenarios. The ICA enables the parties to resort to liquidation, administration, receivership and other available statutory mechanisms together with the ICA or separately. Dealing contractually with the agency costs and strategic creditor actions is rational because e.g. covenant restrictions and standstill clauses and monitoring rights in the financing documentation are likely to lower the cost of capital for the firm; see Armour and Frisby, 'Rethinking Receivership' 80–81.

110 See for the theoretical analysis: Lehtimaki, *Intercreditor agreement as a contractual solution to restructuring leveraged buyouts* Part B.

111 Also, less strict covenant-triggers for the creditor control operate in a similar manner, giving the fund leverage and time should distress ensue.

At first sight, such flexibility would not appear to affect the GP-LP dynamics because both are intended to increase fund value and bargaining leverage.

The incentives resulting from the use of such provisions on the Investment Game become clear when the debtor group is restructured or sold e.g. to a creditor-led new group. The existing private equity fund is in most cases unlikely to reinvest or invest more in the restructured entity due to investment policy restrictions. However, this does not prohibit affiliated funds and or firms from providing the required capital and liquidity. They have after all best knowledge of the business and may hold negotiation leverage against the creditors in the restructuring negotiations. There are naturally various safeguards against affiliated transactions both in the intercreditor documentation and it the LPAs. However, the opaqueness of private benefits of the fund its affiliated entities and the management as well as non-aligned investment opportunities effect the effort decision of the fund management in a distress scenario.

Therefore, it is important that the Investment Game reflects the financial risk-allocation dynamics of an LBO arrangement and deals with the LBO restructuring dynamics and incentives resulting from the financing agreements and the intercreditor agreement.

3.4.2 The Statutory Perspective on Transactions with Affiliated Parties

On the statutory level these concerns are alleviated by the conflicts of interests rules discussed in section 3.1.3, but in order to deal with the risk of transfers between affiliated parties, we can question the necessity of regulating various inducements received from or paid to affiliated parties and third parties.

According to the AIFMR, the *fund manager* is not considered acting prudently, justly and in the interests of the fund investors, if the *fund manager* either receives or pays inducements in connection with management of the fund.[112] However, a number of inducements are excluded from the scope of this restriction, for example, inducements paid to the *fund* or to a person acting on the its behalf and inducements paid by the *fund* or a person acting on its behalf.[113] This means that any payments should be made on the *fund* level. The exception is connected to the requirement to disclose to the LPs any fees and payments as well as the accounts of the fund, avoiding opaqueness of inducements that may be paid to or by some other parties than the fund itself.[114]

---

112 Article 24 of the AIFMR.

113 Ibid, subsection (a).

114 See Articles 22–23 of the AIFMD. It should be noted that Article 18 of the AIFMD obligated the fund manager to maintain and keep available evidence of any transactions entered

The second exception are inducements paid by the *fund manager* to third parties or paid by such a party to the fund manager if the nature and specifics have been disclosed to the LPs prior to the LPs having committed to the fund and the inducement enhances the quality and does not prohibit the fund manager for acting in the interests of the fund and the LPs.[115] Publication of such information in summary form is possible if the fund manager agrees to publish detailed information on the inducements upon separate investor request. Also, normal custody and settlement fees and equivalent fees that cannot lead to conflicts of interest are allowed.[116]

Consequently, to the extent the payments are disclosed and made on the fund level, they are not limited, unless being in breach of 'excessive fees' restricted by the AIFMD or falling within the compensation regulation discussed in section 3.1.3. In practice, the fund management agreement and the advisory agreement as well as the LPA already regulate such payments and fees. In addition, as they are well-understood by institutional LPs, lack of contractual clauses would logically be priced into the required return of the fund pre-investment.

3.5 *Key Propositions for the Investment Game*

There are a number of propositions can we derive from the above analysis for the Investment Game.

1. The question of adverse selection is not as pronounced in the GP-LP relationship, whereas the hidden effort problem is key to the analysis.
2. The key variable in the Investment Game should be the level of effort by the GP and the management team, which rationally correlates with the success of the fund and the LPs.
3. The fundamental objective of private equity funds to reduce management agency costs means that the portfolio company management's incentives are largely aligned with those of the fund.[117]

---

by the fund to ensure compliance of the fund management with the rules of the fund and the applicable law.

115 AIFM Article 24 1(b). Payments in the ordinary course of business, such as depository and settlement fees and similar payments arising in the normal fund management operations are also allowed under a separate exception under Article 24 1(c).

116 Article 24 of the AIFMR.

117 However, the conclusion does not hold (an issue not addressed in this paper) in a distress scenario where the management's incentives may shift towards those of the creditors See e.g. Paterson, 'The Paradox of Alignment: Agency Problems and Debt Restructuring' 511.

4. Any fees and compensation received by the GP and its affiliated parties from transactions and from the portfolio companies are likely to cause misalignment with the LPs.[118]
5. The same applies to any private benefits when a portfolio group becomes distressed, especially if the bargaining leverage of the fund is capable of being used for the advantage of the private equity group as a whole.
6. The opacity of the private benefits within the private equity 'risk allocation space' means that *ex ante* incentivisation of the GP and the fund management may not work and the Investment Game will need to consider independent and effort-based private benefits of the GP and the managers.
7. Therefore, the Investment Game is first and foremost a *maximisation problem* based on the interplay between the hidden effort problem, management agency costs and GP incentivisation through contractual compensation mechanisms.

The equilibria and the maximisation analysis in this Section 4 is based materially on the model and solutions presented by Oren Sussman in Oxford.[119]

4 Game-Theoretical Analysis

4.1 *Introduction*

The Investment Game concerns a scenario where a GP is setting up a fund, the LPs consider making equity investments into the fund and committing to it for ca. 10 years after which the GP makes an effort decision concerning the investment stage and then concerning the exit stage. Increased efforts by the GP and the management team increase the likelihood of a good outcome. The GP and the management team receive private benefits and economic compensation from the fund. The game analyses the conditions under which the GP and the management team are incentivised put in high effort into the fund maximising the LP income.

118 This GP and management compensation structure is naturally a part of the LPA and the fund structure, so technically such compensation are not undisclosed private monetary or non-pecuniary benefits, but part of the incentivisation. However, some of the benefits, such as transaction fees, restructuring benefits, compensation, which may be covered by the contracts, cannot be determined in advance.

119 Notes and materials on the First Principles of Financial Economics, Oxford 2019. Possible mistakes and omissions are my own.

In order to be able to evaluate the parties' strategies, we need to structure the game taking into consideration the alternatives available to the parties and financial outcomes at every stage of the game.[120] We first assume that the players of the game are rational in their decisions, which means that they aim to maximise their personal benefits. In addition, we will assume that the game structure corresponds on a general level to the private equity fund and contractual structures as well as incentives set out in the preceding sections 2 and 3.[121] However, it should be noted that the Investment Game does not address all features governing of the parties' relationship, but only some of the main incentives and conflicts.[122]

This enables us to analyse whether it has any natural equilibria, whether Nash equilibria, sub-game perfect equilibria or some type of a stricter form of equilibria. After the equilibrium analysis, we can evaluate how the parties can maximise their outcome, i.e. whether the equilibria can be Pareto improved. This also enables us to find the specific decision-points that can be governed by contractual clauses or regulation.

4.2 *The General Structure of the Investment Game*

Let's assume that the Investment Game is dynamic[123] game of complete[124] but imperfect[125] information. The fact that the game is a dynamic one with imperfect information means that there are some decision-nodes where a party, here in practice the limited partner (LP), does not know what the General Partner (GP) has decided. The uncertainty concerns the level of effort (π^i) and the undisclosed private benefits (b^i). The uncertainty results in the need to divide

120 We should note here that the bargaining scenario, actual investment, effort during the investment period, fortunes and financial standing of the portfolio companies, as well as the parties' information about the potential outcomes are different from each other.

121 This refers e.g. to typical contractual clauses employed in such relationships and the basic provisions of corporate and insolvency law that set the stage for the decisions in practice. The scope of the institutional framework will, however, necessarily result in high level of generalisation for the game. However, this should be justified taking into consideration that the article is aimed at presenting the recurring incentive conflicts in the presented relationships for the purposes of enhancing private equity regulation.

122 However, focusing especially on the hidden action and agency costs problems should highlight the central features of investment decisions and whether they require to be statutorily regulated.

123 'Dynamic' here means that the game proceeds in stages.

124 'Complete' refers here to the fact that all stakeholders know the possible outcomes of all of the strategies. This aspect of the game will become apparent in the formal analysis.

125 'Imperfect' means in this context that the parties do not necessarily know the decisions of the other parties when making its own decision.

the Investment Game into 'sub-games'. Each sub-game starts from a decision node which is a 'singleton' decision node, i.e. where the party making the decision has a complete and perfect information of the preceding game. All 'non-singeton' decision nodes are the ones connected to another point(s) with a dashed line.[126] The game structure is set out below in figure 3.

The objective of the game is to find outcome maximising equilibria solutions for the Investment Game. This refers to equilibria which would follow were the parties act economically rationally to maximise their outcomes. We assume this to be the case because the parties in the model are sophisticated investors and fund management professionals employing advanced financial models in their decisions.[127]

The Investment Game is an extensive form game. The first terms are the strategy sets of each player. The strategy set of a player consists of all of the strategies of a player: $s_i \in S_i$. The outcomes of various strategies are denoted as 'u', which is the utility of a player, i.e. the outcome of the strategies. The Nash equilibrium in the game is defined formally as: $u_i(s_1^*,\ldots,s_{i-1}^*,s_i^*,\ldots s_{i+1}^*,\ldots s_n^*) \gg u_i(s_1^*,\ldots,s_{i-1}^*,s_i,\ldots s_{i+1}^*,\ldots s_n^*)$. The left side of the equation constitutes the Nash equilibrium because it strictly dominates any other strategy.[128] This means that strategy s_i^* is the best alternative strategy of 'i' by that player considering the best strategies of the other players. The objective of the Investment Game is to find the s_i^* strategies of the players that maximise the utility of the players.

---

126 Such a point means that a party making a decision at that point does not know of the previous decision by the other party. In the Investment Game the opaqueness concerns the effort decision of the GP.

127 Technically, were are trying to find equilibria that are sub-game perfect, i.e. they constitute a Nash equilibrium in every sub-game. 'Nash equilibrium' refers here to a scenario where, for every possible strategy of a player, the actions are chosen in a way that no player can increase its own expected payoff by changing its strategy while the other players keep their strategies unchanged. Despite the fact that there is certain uncertainty in the outcomes, levels of effort and private benefits, the game is structured in the way that we do not have to necessarily evaluate stronger form of equilibria, such as Bayesian equilibrium or Perfect Bayesian equilibrium. However, it should be noted that for quantitative and formal analysis of actual private equity and investment data, the algorithms will have to be modified to reflect the probabilistic nature of the choices.

128 The same inequality can be applied, in addition to s_i to the strategies of all other players as well, *mutatis mutandis*.

4.3 *Game Parameters and Assumptions*

4.3.1 The Parameters

The basic parameters of the game are set out below:

Players (P^i):	the Fund manager or GP (P^{GP}:) and the Limited partner (P^{LP})
y^n:	the fund cash flows, net revenue (management fee and normalised transaction fees deducted)
y^{Alt}:	opportunity cost of the time and effort by the fund management team (net present value)
w:	the funds invested into the fund by the P^{GP} (total investments: 1)
(1 – w):	the funds invested into the fund by the P^{LP} (total investments: 1)
r^h:	the hurdle rate (%) of the fund
R:	the LP investment plus the hurdle rate (r^h)
r:	the opportunity cost rate (rate of return earned on an equivalent alternative investment)
D_δ:	Withdrawal (penalty) (percentage) at the first withdrawal stage
δ:	Discount factor in the withdrawal stage
δ^2:	Discount factor in the final outcomes stage

e^i:	level of effort and skill employed on the fund by the P^{GP}
e^H:	high level of effort and skill employed by the P^{GP}
e^L:	low level of effort and skill employed by the P^{GP}
π^i:	likelihood of a good outcome for the fund subject to (s.t.) the effort of the P^{GP} (applies both to the investment stage and the exist stage)
π^H:	likelihood of a good outcome with high effort by the P^{GP}
π^L:	likelihood of a good outcome with low effort by the P^{GP}
b^i_{GP}:	the level of private benefits for P^{GP}
b^{TrE}:	private benefits for P^{GP} that include possible exceptional transaction fees
b^{TrN}:	private benefits for P^{GP} that include possible normalised transaction fees
b^{Mf}:	private benefits for P^{GP} that include management fees

4.3.2 Assumptions and the Maximisation Problem

The general assumptions, relationships, constants and the outcomes are set out below.[129]

$y\pi^H - e^H > y\pi^{H/L} - e^{H/L} > y\pi^L - e^L$	(1), higher effort less its cost results in increased likelihood of a positive outcome
$\pi^H > \pi^{H/L} > \pi^L$	(2), likelihood of success increases with higher effort
$c_{GP} + c_{LP} = 1$	(3) the fund excess is divided between the GP and the LPs
$R\pi^i = (1 - w)(1 + r)$	(4) the participation constrain of an LP is that it receives at least the estimated (weighted) average of alternative risk rate of return on its investment. For this purpose we assume that the competitive environment causes the rate to level at the level of an alternative risk investment
$w \ll (1 - w)$	(5) LPs investment constitutes a clear majority of the total investment, w being marginal
$R = (1 - w)(1 + r^h)$	(6) The LP return from the fund is the initial investment returned in full plus the hurdle rate
$y \rightarrow \textit{success of the project, i. e.}\ y \geq R$	(7)
$y < R \rightarrow \textit{failure of the project}$	(8)
$e^{L/L} = 0; e^{H/L} = \frac{1}{2} * e^H$	(9) The effort of a low + low situation is scaled to zero for ease of comparison. The efforts of each exit stage are considered having and equal impact, i.e. each contributes on half to the full effort sum e^H
$b^H > b^{H/L} > b^{L/L}$	(10) Transaction fees depend on the effort but accrue with all effort levels. Because transaction fees do not directly depend on the effort, we are able to put them in order, but not scale them.
$\pi^L b^{TrE} = 0$	(11) Low effort results in zero exceptional transaction efforts.

129 Assumptions 1–2, 4, 7–8 are based to a large extent on Notes and materials on the First Principles of Financial Economics, Oxford 2019 by Oren Sussman.

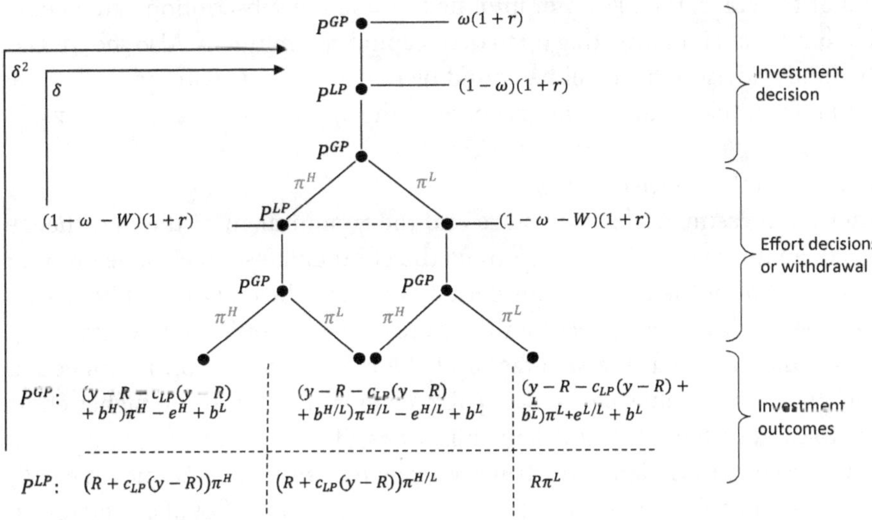

FIGURE 3 The investment game

4.4 *Game Structure and Payoffs*

The strategies and the payoffs of each P^i are set out in figure 3.

4.4.1 The Investment Decision Stage

The GP decides in the first stage whether to establish the fund. The total amount of investments of is scaled to 1 and the GP is able to invest the amount of ω into the fund. The remaining $(1 - \omega)$ is sought from the investors (LPs). The alternative of the GP is investing ω into another same risk-class asset yielding the opportunity cost interest rate, i.e the outcome from that decision is $\omega(1 + r)$. We assume that $1 - \omega \gg \omega$, i.e. the LP investment constitutes the majority of the total investment.[130] However, a large part of the GP opportunity cost is forego-ing the possibility to put its effort to other projects.

The first vertical line represents GPs own investment into the fund and offering the remaining fund units to the investors. The second node represents the LPs investment decision. The decision tree for all LPs is similar.[131] The opportunity cost of investing into the fund is investing into comparable risk rate asset with the outcome $(1 - \omega)(1 + r)$. These decisions can be considered near simultaneous, and no discount factor is applied between these decisions. At the

130 GP Investments are typically on the level of 1–5% of the total investments. I will omit the effect of this investment in the analysis.

131 This means the game can be simplified from a multi-party game to a two-party game.

end of the stage, the LPs enter into the LPA and the subscription agreements that bind them into investing up to their capital commitment. Also the GP and the fund's advisory firm will be bound by the agreements with no walk-away option from the arrangement except with the approval of unanimous LPs.[132]

4.4.2 Effort Decision Stage

After the investment decision stage and the commitment of the LPs, the GP makes an internal decision concerning the effort and resources to be put into management of the fund.[133] This period lasts until the end of the LPA investment period. The alternatives for the GP are high effort (e^H) and low effort (e^L). We assume here that the skill-factor of the management team is embedded into the effort variable, i.e. more capable team is able to provide higher effort and to exert high level of fiduciary obligations.[134]

We assume that high effort is more likely to lead to a good outcome (π^H) than low effort. Conversely, low effort results in a likelihood π^L of a good result. We assume here that $y\pi^H - e > y\pi^L$, i.e. outcome based on high effort, deducting the costs of such higher effort, exceeds the outcome based on lower effort.

The fund is assumed to be under a quarterly and annual fund level and transaction disclosure obligations set out in the fund contracts and side-agreements.[135] Therefore, the LPs have visibility to the economics of the fund, i.e. its investments, selected portfolio company data, withdrawals and leverage. The LPs have a standard option to default or withdraw from the investment commitment. However, this is invariably subject to a heavy sanction in the LPA, e.g. 30% of the value of the calculated level of *pro rata* investments. This withdrawal factor is denoted as D_δ. The net amount received by the respective

132 Sam Kay: Private Equity Fund Structures in Hale, *Private Equity: A Transactional Analysis, Fourth Edition* 53.

133 It is clear that the GP has expressed its level of commitment, the key persons, the management team, its allocated time and past experience with regard to fund management. However, these statements are not as a rule backed by a 'credible threat' in the LPAs. It should be noted, however, that the LPA (fund) GP and advisory firm compensation mechanisms align a part of the incentives of the GP, the managers and the LPs on a financial level. However, we will put this aspect of a 'credible threat' to one side for now.

134 See for a general analysis: Christoph Kaserer and Christian Diller, 'What Drives Private Equity Returns? – Fund Inflows, Skilled GPs, and/or Risk? (February 2007)' Available at SSRN: https://ssrncom/abstract=665602 or http://dxdoiorg/102139/ssrn665602 accessed 5 March 2021.

135 See e.g. for industry standard expectations: ILPA, *ILPA Principles 3.0: Fostering Transparency, Governance and Alignment of Interests for General and Limited Partners* 75–76.

LP is them discounted to the investment decision moment with the discount factor δ, i.e. the discounted outcome for the LP is $(1 - \omega - D_{\delta})\delta$.[136]

The fund subsequently enters into the exist-stage in which the GP makes another effort-decision the effects on the likelihood of a good outcome are similar to the ones set out above in relation to the investment stage. Exit stage effort and skill deviate somewhat from those in the investment stage, so I have considered GP efforts in the two stages separately.[137] For simplicity, we assume that there will be no LP withdrawals during that stage, because the period will end in liquidation, i.e. the economics are the same.

4.4.3 Fund Liquidation Stage

The final stage of the formal analysis involves distribution of the fund assets and profits and closing of the fund. The parties have no withdrawal or effort decisions to make at this point. There are four different outcome alternatives. One for high likelihood of a good outcome (π^H) both in the investment and exist stages. Two for medium likelihood (π^H and π^L in the investment and exist stages) of a good outcome. The final alternative is low likelihood of a good outcome (π^L in both stages).

The bottom part of figure 3 sets out the outcomes for the LPs and the GP in all scenarios. For the GP the all-high effort cases yields to the net sum of the total fund value (y^n) less the LP investment and the hurdle rate (R), added with the 'carry',[138] which is the relative share of the GP for the fund excess over R, i.e. c_{GP} $(y - R)$ added with 'exceptional transaction income' of the GP[139] (high effort outcome). The sum of these items is multiplied with the likelihood of attaining these with high effort (e^h).[140] The cost of effort is deducted from the

136 D_{δ} takes into consideration the fact that the proportional reduction in the funds is calculated from and according to the fund valuation rules set out in the LPA. No fund profit is calculated here because it has not materialised yet.

137 There are also certain additional factors supporting separate treatment. One such factor is that GPs and the management team are often restricted from opening new funds or committing significant time to a new fund before e.g. 70% of the fund assets have been invested. This means that it is in practice likely that the same management team devotes considerable effort on the new fund formation and investment commitments during the exit stage of the earlier fund.

138 The formal model does not deal with so-called 'catch-up' by the GP separately.

139 Because fund investments or exists cannot be carried out without incurring transaction fees, technically it can also be argued that transaction fees should be excluded from the calculation. However, such fees can be a material source of income for groups of which private equity and asset management constitute one part. Therefore, transaction fees are included in the formal analysis as private benefits of the GP and the advisory firm.

140 We assume here that the total excess $(y - R)$ is divided between the GP and the LPs so that $c_{GP} + c_{LP} = 1$. The market for the level of GP carry is usually 20%, so the relative proportions for the GP and the LPs are 20% and 80% respectively.

outcome but the guaranteed management fee b^{Mf} and 'normalised' transaction fees b^{TrN} added, because they accrue independent of effort.[141] Therefore, the GP receives both a part of the profit and additional fees from the fund.

If the combination of the investment stage and exit stage includes both high and low effort, these are considered interchangeable. In that case the likelihood of success is lower ($\pi^{H/L}$). Otherwise the equation is similar to that of high effort.

The low/low effort situation resembles the previous equations, but it should be noted that, due to the earlier assumptions (7) and (8) factor $(y - R)$ is negative and the GP outcome is reduced to $b^{Tr}\pi^{L} + b^{L}$.

The outcomes for the LPs are more straightforward. The basic income, i.e. repayment of capital plus the hurdle rate (total of R) is added with the LPs' share of the excess of the distributable net income after payment of R. The general outcome for the LPs is $R + c_{LP}(y - R)\pi^{i}$, depending on the effort decisions of the GP in the two stages. It should be noted that in the low/low effort scenario $(y - R) < 0$ in which case the outcome is limited to $R\pi^{L}$ and there is no excess to be distributed, neither to the LPs nor the GP.[142]

4.5 *The Equilibria and Maximisation Analysis*

In order for the LPs to be able to ensure the GP puts in high effort into the fund, defusing the moral hazard problem, the LPs will have to solve the GPs income maximisation game. This means that the LPs et their own income rate R in such a way that ensures that GP and the management team give all-high effort.

For this purpose, we will take a look at the game which consist, in relation to the GP, of two sub-games. It is necessary to solve the equilibria and maximisation problem of the sub-games first.[143]

4.5.1 The GP Game

4.5.1.1 *The Relative Analysis between Different GP Effort Levels*

The first GP sub-games starts after the LP investment decision and the second GP sub-game starts in the effort-decision stage of the exit-stage. In order to use backward induction to the sub-games, we need to analyse first the outcomes.

141 I have assumed that parties affiliated to the GP are able to charge for the transactions. This will not hold in all scenarios but is assumed to hold in the Investment Game.

142 It is naturally possible the capital of the fund is partially or wholly lost. However, this feature is taken into consideration in setting π^{i}.

143 Sub-games can only start in the nodes, where there is full information. Therefore, sub-games cannot start in the initial first decision node or in decision-nodes, which are connected by dashed lines.

Substituting assumption (3), (6),[144] (9) and (11) into the three GP outcomes, we get:

The general outcome equation: $(y^n - R - c_{LP}(y^n - R) + b^{TrE})\,\pi^i - e^i + b^{Mf} + b^{TrN}$

$A^0: c_{GP}\pi^H(y^n - (1 - \omega)(1 + r)) + \pi^H b^{TrE} + b^{Mf} + e^H$ (all high effort)

$B^0: c_{GP}\pi^{\frac{H}{L}}(y^n - (1 - \omega)(1 + r)) + \pi^{H/L} b^{TrE} + b^{Mf} + b^{TrN} - \frac{1}{2}e^H$ (high-low effort)

$C^0: c_{GP}\pi^L(0) + \pi^L b^{TrE} + b^{Mf} + b^{TrN} - 0 \rightarrow \pi^L b^{TrE} + b^{Mf} + b^{TrN}$[145] (all low effort)

The explanation of equations A and B is straight-forward. The relative outcomes depend on:

(i) the effort-based likelihood of obtaining
  a. the 'carry part' of the 'excess' over LP distributions; and
  b. the extraordinary transaction income; and

(ii) the size of the cost of the effort.

Management fees and regular transaction fees do not affect the relative outcomes directly, because they accrue irrespective of effort in all scenarios.[146] However, they may still affect the relative outcomes if b^i is high-enough (and because b^i is more certain than the good fund outcome with high-effort) and if e^i grows significantly between the effort levels. Despite assumption (1) which ensures that higher effort will lead to higher outcome even if the cost of effort rises, there is a possibility that the GP is incentivised to set up new and parallel funds with same and lower effort while relying on b^i in all of the managed funds, leading to very high private benefits. This question is put aside in this analysis because LPAs usually require that the managers spend a majority of their time on a particular fund up to e.g. 70% investment threshold and,

144 This aligns the outcomes with the assumption that the provision of LP funding is ample and is offered by the institutional investor base up to the level the return equals that of comparable same risk-level investments (r).

145 The low-low outcome consists of the management fee, normal transaction income and low likelihood exceptional transaction income. The equation is scaled so that is does not lead to a 'carry' for the GP or the fund managers.

146 However, as set out in the below section, they affect the rate setting and equilibrium conditions.

secondly, because the managers and the LPs would face a similar problem question in the other fund as well.[147]

Assuming (1), we see that the order of the outcomes is $(A^0) > (B^0) > (C^0)$, unless $\frac{e^H}{2} > \Delta\pi c_{GP}(y-R) + \Delta\pi b^{TrN}$. This means the all-high effort prevails if the growth in the GP's income and exceptional transaction fees is greater than the growth in GP effort cost between different effort levels.[148]

4.5.1.2 *Graphical Analysis*

The relationship between different outcomes becomes clear when we present them graphically. The x-axis in the below graphs represents the rate of *R*, i.e. the share of the assets and profit distributed to the LPs and the y-axis represents the income of the GP and its affiliated entities. The effort levels are plotted against different levels of *R*.[149]

Acting rationally, GP is likely to choose the effort level providing the highest outcome for a given *R*, i.e. the share paid to the LPs. The graphs show that the optimal effort-level changes as a function of *R*. The higher the ratio paid |to the LPs, assuming for now that the private benefits and costs remain fixed, the higher the likelihood of lower effort by the GP.

Plots 4b and 4c represent the same GP game and outcomes in the final stage. However, how they differ from figure 4a is that they show how different levels of private benefits b^i affect the effort equilibria and the GPs choice of optimal effort level for the fund.

---

147 The effects of managing multiple funds in connection with the Investment Game would also require additional research on the income dynamics of such fund structures.

148 We can alternatively take a look at the relative outcomes of the two first effort-scenarios. We can see under what conditions the high-high effort yields higher outcome than the high-low effort by deducting the first from the latter and seeing under which conditions the equation is larger than zero: $(c_{GP}(y^n - R) + b^{TrE}) \sim (e^H + e^{\frac{H}{L}}) / (\pi^H + \pi^{\frac{H}{L}}) \rightarrow (c_{GP}(y^n - R) + b^{TrE}) \sim (1\frac{1}{2}e^H) / \Delta\pi$. Therefore, the determining factor is the relation between the level of costs and the difference of likelihood in obtaining a good fund outcome. The high-high effort outcome is larger if the left-hand side of the equation is greater than the right-hand side. Noting that most of the factors in the equations are case-specific so the solution always depends on such items, we need to focus on the most important questions for the game: the size of *R* and relationship between the total costs of effort and the difference in the likelihood of attaining the good outcome in the evaluated scenarios.

149 The analysis was carried out by using Mathematica software.

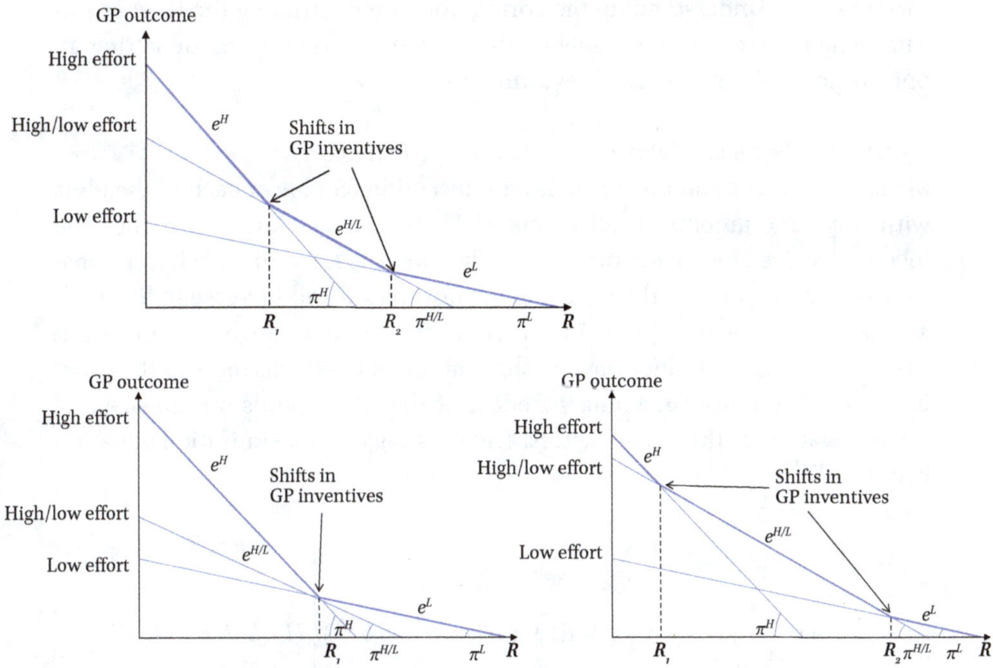

FIGURES 4A, 4B AND 4C Shifts in GP incentives based on *R*

There are several points to note in the above figures. We can see in figure 4a that the angle of the high-effort (e^H) alternative is steeper than for the high-low effort ($e^{H/L}$) alternative and the angle of the high-low effort alternative is steeper than of the low-low effort (e^L) alternative. As a result, the plots are likely to intersect for certain values of R.[150] At these points GP will be indifferent whether to give a high or low effort to the fund.[151] Beyond this intersection point, a higher R may result a lower effort by the GP and lower likelihood of a good outcome for the LPs.

The private benefits received by the GP raise or lower the plot lines, affecting the point where the incentive to give high effort changes to an incentive to give a lower effort. However, because the effort (e^i) and the likelihood of good outcome (π^i) are connected, looking just at the effects of effort and cost is not sufficient. Their impact on the equilibrium levels of R depend on their

150 Whether there exist intersection points, depends on case-specific effort levels, cost of effort, carry rate, LP rate and the private benefit items received by the GP. For analytical purposes, the model assumed such intersections take place. However, in the end this depends on empirical analysis.

151 The relative level of cost-to effort changes the angle and height (up or down) of the plot lines.

correlation.[152] Understanding the correlation and controlling the level of private benefits is material for solving the Investment Game, i.e. for setting an optimal level of R in an actual investment scenario.

4.5.1.3 *The Effect of Private Benefits on Optimal Effort*

Management fees and the normalised transaction fees lower each of the plots with the same amount at all points.[153] These changes lower or reduce the income received by the GP and conversely lower the LP returns.[154] Exceptional transaction fees are, on the other hand, effort-based and increase in line with π^i. Their existence adds to the incentives of the GP to use higher effort, but at the same time, they reduce the LPs' share of the fund returns more as the effort increases. The output maximising effort of the GP depends on the size and the correlation of the above factors. The GP subgame maximisation equation becomes:[155]

$$argmax_{i\in\left\{L,\frac{H}{L},H\right\}}(c_{GP}\pi^i(y^n-R)+\pi^i b^{TrE}+b^{Mf}+b^{TrN} -e^i)=\begin{cases} H \text{ if } R\leq R_1 \\ H/L \text{ if } R_1\leq R\leq R_2 \\ L \text{ if } R\leq R_2 \end{cases}$$

[GP subgame maximisation solution = S^{*Sub}]

S^{*Sub} is the solution to the GPs output maximisation problem in the sub-game. It tells us on what level of LP return rate the GP gives high effort to the fund. The equation is a formal representation of figures 4a, 4b and 4c.

152 Any actual, more detailed, correlation analysis requires statistical analysis of private equity market data, which is subject to further research.

153 These items are not effort dependent. However, there is a valid argument that also normalised transaction fees can be effort-dependent, and a good management team is able to originate more and better transactions, which is undoubtedly the case. However, these factors are also accounted for as a part of the exceptional transaction fees. Their relationship remains subject to further empirical analysis.

154 However, these benefits may naturally be so high, especially with funds with high levels of assets under management, that the managers deem the income level sufficient compensate for a low effort level. However, the game assumes that the GP will aim to maximise its effort and cost-based profit, i.e. still put in high effort if economically rational.

155 The maximisation argument here is based on the structure and analysis by Oren Sussman, Notes and materials on the First Principles of Financial Economics, Oxford 2019. Possible mistakes and omissions are my own.

In addition to the effort decisions in the two stages in figure 3, the Investment Game includes only one additional decision-node for the GP because it cannot withdraw (except for certain very non-beneficial situations) from the fund. Therefore, from the GP decision-point-of-view, the relevant comparison is between the discounted outcome in the final stage and the initial fund formation decision, i.e. $\omega(1 + r) + y^{Alt}$. S^{*Sub} exceeds this level unless the discount factor δ^2 is very high or if y^{Alt} overrides discounted A^0 Because $w \ll (1 - w)$ and because r represent market rate (and the fund seeks to yield alpha), w or r are unlikely to outweigh the discounted outcome of A^0, i.e. the subgame-perfect outcome.

The more likely factor capable of outweighing A^0 is the net present value of alternative use of management time and effort y^{Alt}. However, the LPs can assume A^0 outweighs y^{Alt} at least up to the level of R and draft contract terms (b^i) proposed by the GP in the first stage. Otherwise the GP would not propose the structure. Because, in the first stage, the LPs know the GPs initial proposal and understand the effort-decision and the private benefits of the GP, LPs are able to calculate the connection between R and the high-effort rate range of the final outcome graphs. The next stage of the analysis is to evaluate what is the best strategy of the LPs to counter the GP's initial fund proposal.

4.5.2 The LP Game

4.5.2.1 *The Relative Analysis between Different Outcomes*

Because the optimal strategy of the GP is determined by factors some of which may be undisclosed or opaque to the LPs, they need to have a strategy that optimises the GP effort to the level delivering the best outcome for the LPs. Because the optimal effort level of the GP can be plotted against the LP return rate R, the LPs can control the effort by negotiating R, setting it high enough without affecting the GP effort decision. However, because some of the private benefits (b^i), such as LBO restructuring benefits and management compensation, are undisclosed or opaque, the LPs will also need to have a strategy for controlling these.

First, let's take a look the LP outcomes in the final stage. In the second equations, I have substituted $R\pi^i$ with assumption (6).

$$(R + c_{LP}(y - R))\pi^H \quad \rightarrow \quad (1 - \omega)(1 + r) + \pi^H c_{LP} y - \pi^H c_{LP} R \qquad (A^0)$$

$$(R + c_{LP}(y - R))\pi^{H/L} \quad \rightarrow \quad (1 - \omega)(1 + r) + \pi^{H/L} c_{LP} y - \pi^{H/L} c_{LP} R \qquad (B^0)$$

$$R\pi^L \quad (C^0)$$

Based on the assumptions (1) and (2), we can see that, unlike with the GP outcome, $(A^0) > (B^0) > (C^0)$ without additional qualifications. This enables us to compare the feasibility of A^0 to the LP outcomes in the investment decision stage and the withdrawal decision stage, all discounted to the initial stage. The outcomes are:

$$[(1-\omega)(1+r) + \pi^H c_{LP} y - \pi^H c_{LP} R]\delta^2 \qquad (D^0)$$

$$(1-\omega^0 - D^\delta)(1+r)\delta \qquad (E^0) \text{ Withdrawal decision stage}$$

$$(1-\omega)(1+r) \qquad (F^0) \text{ Investment decision stage}$$

Before solving the maximisation problem, we need to note a few points. First, LPs cannot directly observe the effort or the likelihood of a successful project or the level of private benefits of the GP. If it were able to observe these *ex ante*, it could fix its return (R) and c_{LP}. However, LPs can determine confidently, through maximisation analysis, the likely actions and effort by the GP and set R optimally and negotiate b^i.

Secondly, private benefits and conflicts of interest will necessarily increase the riskiness of the fund, i.e. also the discount factor δ. Because term of the fund is ca. 10 years, δ will be a significant factor when making the decision. This leaves us the strategy of setting a correct R and negotiating the treatment of the private benefits and conflict scenarios into the LPA.

Because of the very high figure of D^δ (e.g. 30%–50% of the entire investment), D^0 *and* $E^0 > F^0$ in almost all cases. Whether D^0 or F^0 is bigger, in turn depends on the discount factor δ^2 (the riskiness of the investment) and π^i i.e. the likelihood of success of the fund. First, the level of δ can be determined on a satisfactory confidence from the PE market data.[156] the Secondly, because π^i correlates directly with e^i,[157] $D^0 > F^0$ with a very high likelihood if the effort level is π^H or $\pi^{H/L}$. Assuming this, the solution to the LP maximisation problem, is D^0, i.e. ensuring π^H.[158] This is the best LP strategy in the Investment Game.

156 We should note that the opaqueness of the fund is connected to its riskiness. This creates an incentive to the GP to disclose b^i to lower the higher R resulting from the higher discount factor of the final outcome.

157 Determining the actual riskiness of the investment requires use of quantitative data together with the model. This enables use of the Investment Game solution in an actual investment decision.

158 It should be noted that a fund-specific analysis always depends on case-specific features and deal terms.

4.5.2.2 *Graphical Analysis of the Outcomes*

I have plotted below the LP outcome subject to GP subgame maximisation solution.

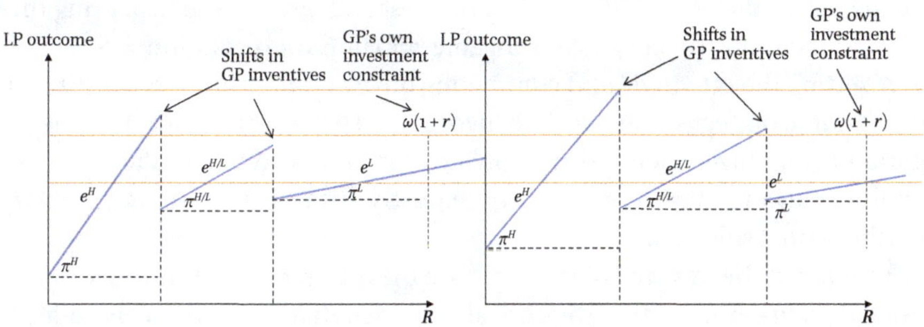

FIGURES 5A AND 5B LP investment outcomes based on e^i

The first conclusion from the above is that the LPs maximise their outcome by ensuring that the GP gives high-high effort. They can do that by setting the total LP return on a level that incentivises this. For example in figure 5b, the highest level (horizontal line) is just achievable by setting R at the first vertical dashed line or slightly below it. Lower levels of effort do not maximise in the figures the LP outcome. The low effort (after the second vertical dashed line in figures 5a and 5b) alternative could theoretically achieve as high an outcome as the high-high alternative, but this is unlikely because the GP opportunity cost on the right means that the GP will not consider fund investment beyond that point. The GP would not set up the fund with those economics.

The second insight is that both the private benefits and the costs of the GP shift the plot lines either up or down (conversely to the GP plot). The changes to the equilibria can be seen from figures 5a and 5b. Figure 5a corresponds otherwise to 5b but higher private benefits by the GP in 5a lower the plot lines overall. This means that in figure 5b, the LPs achieve higher outcome levels with same level of R compared to figure 5a. In addition to the outcome levels, the shift also has an impact (depending on the level of total private benefits) on the points where the incentive of the GP to give higher effort shifts to lower effort.[159]

159 The management fee is the only private benefit that the LPs are able to control directly. The level of transaction fees (including affiliated company benefits) cannot be predetermined. Because, unlike with the cost of effort which is connected to the likelihood of a good outcome, private benefits do not have a direct link to the success of the fund, the

Therefore, LPs will either:
(i) have to know these benefits and costs *ex ante*, and/or
(ii) be able to control them contractually.
Otherwise the LPs cannot set the correct or optimal level of R despite being able to control the effort. This leads to the best strategy of LP, considering the best strategy (and subject to GP subgame maximisation solution = S^{*Sub}) of GP, of setting the rate to R^* and contracting on b^i *ex ante*. This also constitutes the sub-game perfect solution of the Investment Game. This is also the general solution to the Investment Game. Solving S^{*Sub} and S^* in a specific case and actual scenario requires the use of PE industry data analytics in connection with the formal solution.

Therefore, if the LPs are able to negotiate the return rate and controls on the private benefits *ex ante*, that they are able to incentivise the GP to give a high effort. This leads to an equilibrium where better effort, fiduciary obligations or statutory liability for suboptimal investment effort would not have to be regulated but would follow from private contracting.

5 Conclusions

The findings of the above section lead to two solutions to the output maximisation problem and, as a result, give an insight on the scope of private equity contracting and fund regulation. The analysis suggests that the hidden effort problem can be managed by the LPs despite the GP not being able to commit credibly to giving certain effort. Secondly, because the LPs assume the existence of b^i, unless they are disclosed or contractually regulated, the LPs will rationally require a higher R – leading to a lower outcome for the GP. Therefore, GPs have an incentive to either disclose or agree on the treatment of b^i, *ex ante*.

This suggests that regulation of inducements and compensation of fund managers discussed in Section 3.2.3 is not feasible because the fund managers are already incentivised to disclose the same. Furthermore, certain items that are economically private benefits may not even be covered by the regulation. The fact that the international LPAs as a rule contain regulation obligating the fund manager to return or pay to the fund any contractually restricted payments, e.g. through reduction in the periodic management fee by way of set-off, supports

evaluation of the level of such fees is different from the effort maximisation problem. With the decision on R, the LPs can ensure that the GP gives necessarily the high-high effort. However, the private benefits are not so connected to R and may accrue irrespective of the likelihood of the good outcome, i.e. effort.

the Investment Game conclusion that the parties are incentivised to agree on such matters *ex ante*, and in fact do that.

However, because the LPs are not always able to coordinate such a solution, the finding is subject to qualifications. This is the case only when the LPs cannot negotiate with the GP or their bargaining leverage is low, i.e. (i) if there is low fund supply and excessive market demand; or (ii) in retail fund offering. However, sophisticated institutional investors are able to analyse the level of the compensation and benefits and, if they are lead investors, to affect the fund terms and the riskiness of the investment policy. They are able to affect the compensation levels provided that either they have individually, or as a collective, negotiating leverage over the terms.

High fund leverage and opaqueness of the LBO financing and restructuring structures mean that the fund may 'step-up in the priority ladder' receiving substantial benefits and interests before the LPs. Private benefits affect the relative distribution of returns of the fund, the riskiness of the investment and comparison to alternative comparable investments. The LPs, acting rationally, also assume under the Investment Game the estimated level of such costs and price them into *R*. This gives the GP and incentive to contract on or disclose such benefits *ex ante*. This incentive is supported by a connected factor of the LPs discounting the fund outcome with a higher discount rate δ, unless they can contract on the opaque private benefits, knowledge of which have an impact on the risk factor. However, unless industry standards develop do deal with this problem, the opaqueness of the LBO is hard to overcome and may require regulatory intervention in relation to funds offered to retail investors or where the LP base is large or fragmented.

The GPs have an enhanced incentive to either disclose or contract on benefits, if a higher *R* needed to compensate the LPs for the opaqueness of the benefits, the effort and the LBO structure, is larger than the costs of committing to disclosure and/or remitting all or part of the benefits to the fund. This means that the answer is really about marginal costs of committing to such a deal in a genuine bargaining scenario – something that can be empirically analysed.[160]

These marginal costs depend on the parties' negotiation leverage. As mentioned in Section 3.3, investment periods of private equity funds are long and fund disclosure or the manager's obligations may not be supported by sufficient remedies. In addition, legislation applying to partnerships often prohibits

160 See Section 3.3. The incomplete contracting claim is unlikely to hinder such effective bargaining. See: Lehtimaki, *Intercreditor agreement as a contractual solution to restructuring leveraged buyouts* Part D.

the LPs' possibilities to affect operation of the fund.[161] Lacking LP negotiation leverage, a large-enough unaffiliated LP, or the possibility of confidently estimating the effects of private benefits and effort means that the hurdle rates may converge to a market standard, e.g. to 8% per annum, instead of a risk-adjusted rate that takes into consideration the hidden action problem and the private benefits or a contractual solution to the same.[162]

However, rational GPs and LPs should follow the logic of the Investment Game. This is because, irrespective of the leverage, with the knowledge of the effort problem and most common private benefits in private equity transactions, LBOs and their effects on the Investment Game, LPs are able to have these costs embedded in their financial models based on the existing data and determine their effects of setting *R*. If they cannot affect the level of *R*, they can negotiate control clauses into the fund documentation. If LPs are able to evaluate the effects of private benefits through data and game theoretical analysis, the GPs will have an enhanced incentive to disclose these benefits *and* credibly commit to either have the LPs decide on these, or account such benefits to the fund. If the Investment Game leads to non-investment, this is not a failure of the private contracting regime, but a normal commercial scenario based on prudent investment analysis. Something that does not require regulatory intervention.

The findings of the Investment Game also mean that the inducements and fee disclosure regulation in the AIFMD lower the costs for the LPs for investing into the fund, but the benefits are likely to be non-material. This is because the LPs enter into the negotiations in a genuine bargaining scenario in any case and imposing additional statutory compliance requirements on private benefits is unlikely to provide the LPs additional protection. The same applies to restrictions on fund manager and portfolio managers' compensation because they can be controlled by LPs (or their collective) that have sufficient leverage in the investment negotiations. Therefore, e.g. exclusion of private equity funds offered to professional investors from the scope of the more detailed performance compensation regulation in the EU[163] is well-founded. Despite

161 See Lin, 'Private Equity in Singapore' 1. See also Limited Partnerships Act (Cap 163B, 2010 Rev Ed) s 6.

162 Therefore, the solution would appear subject to possibility of private contracting or, failing that, fund regulation or extension of investment manager's fiduciary duties under law. In relation to effects of lack of fiduciary duties in private equity and venture capital, see: Tan, 'FIDUCIARY DUTIES IN THE PRIVATE EQUITY AND VENTURE CAPITAL WORLD'. Failing to agree on the private benefits the LP return rate is likely converge to industry standard, i.e. not reflecting the economic fundamentals or the riskiness of the fund.

163 ESMA Guidelines on performance fees in UCITS and certain types of AIFS, ESMA34-39-992, 5/11/2020.

the contractual challenges, LPAs are in practice heavily negotiated and they contain several compromises and solutions that deal with the maximisation problem. There are usually also lead investors that are able to negotiate a sensible economic solution to these issues. Also, the market standard LPA disclosure and reporting clauses are extensive and provide extensive reporting on the fund economics and portfolio economics. This supports the Investment Game conclusions that LPs are, indeed, in most cases able to determine these issues *ex ante* and, the GPs are rational in adapting to this. In such a case, disclosure regulation would not yield additional benefits to the investors, and resorting to the 'incomplete contracting' claim would not be a rational argument. Although, the objective of this paper is not to discuss, whether regulatory intervention based on an incomplete contracting claim is justifiable, it should be noted the private equity contracts are heavily negotiated and evidence a sophisticated bargaining game between the parties governing all of the most important scenarios.[164]

Importantly, the level of investor fragmentation has led, although not due to only these reasons, e.g. the Institutional Limited Partners Association ("ILPA") to produce best practises to improve private equity industry for the long-term benefit of all stakeholders.[165] For example ILPA Principles 3.0 (2019) provide comprehensive 'soft law' regulation to address the discussed issues in LPAS such as conflicts of interests, private benefits, GP incentivisation, transparency and several other features of structuring and management of funds and their investments. However, such rules appear rather to codify rather than to create more transparent solutions already provided by the Investment Game.[166] From the regulatory perspective, it may therefore be a better alternative to require in the retail markets at least the equal protections afforded to institutional LPs in negotiated fund offerings. Despite some qualifications to the solutions of the Investment Game, the findings are important e.g. to the Chief Investment Officer of the example scenario discussed in the beginning. With access to private equity fund data and contractual databases, the pension insurance company can use the Investment Game embedded with this data for actually solving a particular investment game.

164 See for the deficiencies of the incomplete contracting claim: Lehtimaki, *Intercreditor agreement as a contractual solution to restructuring leveraged buyouts* Part D 4(c).

165 ILPA, *ILPA Principles 3.0: Fostering Transparency, Governance and Alignment of Interests for General and Limited Partners.*

166 Although being an industry association promoting mainly the interests of the LPs, their fundamental principles provide support for contracting in the LPAs about these issues and the concerns of the investor community. This is not surprising, because negotiation leverage can also be achieved, not only by large-enough investors, but industry organisations that have collective force to effect the same.

Acknowledgments

The author would like to thank and is grateful to the Centre for Banking & Finance Law at National University of Singapore, Faculty of Law, for funding this research project and for supporting the conduct of this research.

Bibliography

Akerlof GA, *The market for "lemons": quality uncertainty and the market mechanism* (1970).

Armour J and Frisby S, 'Rethinking Receivership' (2001) 21 Oxford Journal of Legal Studies 73.

Axelson U and others, 'Borrow Cheap, Buy High? The Determinants of Leverage and Pricing in Buyouts' 68 Journal of Finance 2223.

Axelson U, Strömberg P and Weisbach MS, 'Why Are Buyouts Levered? The Financial Structure of Private Equity Funds' (2009) LXIV Journal of Finance 1549.

Baird DG, Gertner RH and Picker RC, *Game Theory and the Law* (Harvard University Press 1994).

Billett MT and others, 'Bank Skin in the Game and Loan Contract Design: Evidence from Covenant-Lite Loans' 51 839.

Billington D, 'Syndicated lending' in Shutter A (ed), *A practitioner's guide to syndicated lending* (Second edn, Sweet & Maxwell 2017).

Brown G and others, 'Private Equity: Accomplishments and Challenges' 32 Journal of Applied Corporate Finance 8.

Coase R, 'The Nature of the Firm' (1937) 4 Economica 386.

Driessen J, Lin T-C and Phalippou L, *A New Method to Estimate Risk and Return of Non-traded Assets from Cash Flows: The Case of Private Equity Funds (February 14, 2011)* (Journal of Financial and Quantitative Analysis (JFQA), Forthcoming, EFA 2007 Ljubljana Meetings Paper, AFA 2008 New Orleans Meetings Paper, Swedish Institute for Financial Research Conference on The Economics of the Private Equity Market).

Gilligan J and Wright M, *Private Equity Demystified, An explanatory guide* (2nd edn, ICAEW Corporate Finance Faculty 2010).

Gilson RJ, 'Engineering a Venture Capital Market: Lessons from the American Experience' 55 Stanford Law Review 1067.

Hale C, *Private Equity: A Transactional Analysis, Fourth Edition* (4th edn, Globe Law and Business 2020).

Haugen R and Senbet L, 'Bankruptcy and Agency Costs: Their Significance to the Theory of Optimal Capital Structure' (1988) 23 Journal of Financial and Quantitative Analysis 27.

ILPA, *ILPA Principles 3.0: Fostering Transparency, Governance and Alignment of Interests for General and Limited Partners* (2019).

Jensen MC and Meckling WH, *Theory of the firm: managerial behavior, agency costs and ownership structure* (1976).

Kaplan SN and Strömberg P, 'Leveraged Buyouts and Private Equity' (2009) 23 Journal of Economic Perspectives 121.

Kaserer C and Diller C, 'What Drives Private Equity Returns? – Fund Inflows, Skilled GPs, and/or Risk? (February 2007)' Available at SSRN: https://ssrncom/abstract=665602 or http://dxdoiorg/102139/ssrn665602 accessed 5 March 2021.

Knoll MS, *The Modigliani-Miller Theorem at 60: The Long-Overlooked Legal Applications of Finance's Foundational Theorem (October 11, 2017)*. (U of Penn, Inst for Law & Econ Research Paper No. 17–43. Available at SSRN: https://ssrn.com/abstract=3053953 2017).

Kraakman RH and others, *The anatomy of corporate law: a comparative and functional approach* (Third edn, Oxford University Press 2017).

Lehtimaki M, *Intercreditor agreement as a contractual solution to restructuring leveraged buyouts* (2020).

Lehtimaki MJ, *Debt subordination in corporate liquidation* (2007).

Lin L, 'Engineering a Venture Capital Market: Lessons from China' 30 Columbia Journal of Asian Law 160.

Lin L, 'Private Equity in Singapore' SSRN Electronic Journal.

Malenko A and Malenko N, 'A theory of LBO activity based on repeated debt-equity conflicts' 117 Journal of Financial Economics 607.

Morris P and Phalippou L, 'Thirty years after Jensen's prediction: is private equity a superior form of ownership?' [Oxford University Press] 36 Oxford Review of Economic Policy.

Myers SC and Majluf NS, *Corporate Financing and Investment Decisions When Firms Have Information That Investors Do Not Have* (National Bureau of Economic Research 1984).

Paterson S, 'The Paradox of Alignment: Agency Problems and Debt Restructuring' 17 European Business Organization Law Review 497.

Payne J, 'Private Equity and Its Regulation in Europe' 12 EUROPEAN BUSINESS ORGANIZATION LAW REVIEW.

Phalippou L, 'Beware of Venturing into Private Equity' 23 Journal of Economic Perspectives 147.

Phalippou L, *The Future of Private Markets (June 30, 2018)* (Available at SSRN: https://ssrn.com/abstract=3170928 2018).

Phalippou L, 'The Future of Private Markets (June 30, 2018)' Available at SSRN: https://ssrncom/abstract=3170928.

Phalippou L, 'Modifying The Carried Interest To Do What It Is Said To Do (February 12, 2019)' Available at SSRN: https://ssrncom/abstract=3333053.

Phalippou L, *An Inconvenient Fact: Private Equity Returns & The Billionaire Factory* (*June 10, 2020*) (University of Oxford, Said Business School, Working Paper 2020).

Phalippou L, Rauch C and Umber M, 'Private equity portfolio company fees' 129 Journal of financial economics 559.

Renneboog L and Vansteenkiste C, 'Leveraged Buyouts: A Survey of the Literature (March 9, 2017)'. CentER Paper Discussion Series No 2017-015.

Repiquet MD, 'A Failed Attempt to Protect Hedge Fund Investors? An Inquiry into the Alternative Investment Fund Managers Directive' 12 Liberty University law review.

Robinson DT and Sensoy BA, 'Do Private Equity Fund Managers Earn Their Fees? Compensation, Ownership, and Cash Flow Performance' 26 The Review of Financial Studies 2760.

Schillig M, 'The Contribution of Law and Economics as a Method of Legal Reasoning in European Private Law' (Alphen aan den Rijn, The Netherlands) 17 European Review of Private Law 853.

Shivdasani A and Wang Y, 'Did Structured Credit Fuel the LBO Boom?' (2011) 66 Journal of Finance 66 1291.

Shutter A, *A practitioner's guide to syndicated lending* (Shutter A ed, Sweet & Maxwell: Thomson Reuters 2010).

Spindler J, 'How Private Is Private Equity?' (Washington) 32 Regulation 38.

Tan CM, 'Fiduciary Duties in the Private Equity and Venture Capital World' 4 International Comparative Jurisprudence 66.

Wood P, *Project finance, securitisations, subordinated debt* (2nd edn, Sweet & Maxwell 2007).

www.ingramcontent.com/pod-product-compliance
Lightning Source LLC
Chambersburg PA
CBHW072244240926
51846CB00012B/608
* 9 7 8 9 0 0 4 5 1 4 6 3 8 *